Give Your Child *Genius IQ*

A program for busy parents

Sidney Ledson

Mentiscopic Publishing Company Ltd.

Canadian Cataloguing in Publication Data

Ledson, Sidney.
    Give your child genius IQ

Includes Index

ISBN: 978-1-4120-9900-4

Mentiscopic Publishing Company Ltd.
46 Minnacote Ave.,
Toronto, ON   M1E 4B3

Order this book online at www.trafford.com or email orders@trafford.com
Most Trafford titles are also available at major online book retailers.

North America & international
toll-free: 1 888 232 4444 (USA & Canada)
phone: 250 383 6864 ♦ fax: 812 355 4082

Trafford rev. 2/02/2010

Contents

1

The Rise and Fall of the Brilliant Child

Considering how easy it is to raise children's intelligence, it's a wonder we're not up to here with Albert Einsteins: an absence made the more puzzling because children are bright to begin with. Two-, three-, and four-year-olds often reveal an intellectual sparkle that parents chatter excitedly about; yet, strangely enough, this initial burst of brilliance diminishes a few years later to the faint glow we term average or normal intelligence – expressed as IQ 100. What happened to the early promise?

Parents sometimes fail to realize that their child's intelligence is easily altered, and that they, the parents, have primary control – first grabs, as it were – in altering that intelligence. When parents fail to exercise their mind-expanding option the world exerts its own leveling influence, one that favors an IQ of 100. Such is the price of leaving a child's intellectual growth to chance.

We have been 'altering' children's intelligence at the Sidney Ledson Institute for Intellectual Advancement since 1980. The descriptions of children's accomplishments seen on pages 185 to 187 reveal the benefits these children and thousands like them have gained. Today, these youngsters – some, now adults – lead expanded lives because of the program on which this book is based. The purpose here is to bring the Institute program to *you* so you may give your child the precious advantages that accompany high intelligence.

What will be your cost in time? Very little. The program is tailored to fit the tight schedule of working parents. The mind-expanding activities are programmed for moments when you deal with routine household chores and while traveling, shopping and eating; in short, a program easily followed by even harried single parents.

1

What teaching experience is needed? None. Children's eager participation is assured by tested motivating procedures. But wait. Take a worst case scenario. Let's suppose you lack confidence, or patience, or for some other reason you simply choose not to teach. Not to worry. You will learn of a little-guessed source of instructional help that guarantees success for your program with minimal contribution by you. Of this, more later. Now to business.

First, let's consider the claim conveyed by the title of this book: genius IQ for your child. What do I mean by *genius IQ*? IQ stands for *intelligence quotient*; this, a verbal ruler that defines levels of intelligence. For example, an IQ of 100 indicates average intelligence – the level of cleverness you normally meet among those you encounter while shopping. Higher IQ numbers indicate higher intelligence. Those who deal with the science of measuring intelligence (psychometricians) – tell us that an IQ of 140 represents the estimated threshold of genius intelligence. Possessing an IQ of 140 or higher places one among the movers and shakers of the world. Einstein, for example, had an estimated IQ of 160. Bill Gates is also rated at 160. Stephen Hawking rates 164, and chess masters Bobby Fisher and Gary Casparov are rated at 187 and 190 respectively.

For children, the IQ number indicates the relationship between a child's age and his or her intellectual performance. To determine a child's IQ level we divide the child's intellectual age by his or her actual age, then multiply the result by one hundred. For example, if we have a three-year-old (thirty-six months) who thinks and behaves like most children a year and a half older than he is (fifty-four months), we would divide the child's mental age (54) by his actual age (36) then multiply the result by one hundred, revealing an IQ of 150 – a very bright child.

Just how easy is it to raise a child's intelligence? You decide. Consider the drama that unfolded in the Markwell* home when their son John was twenty-one months old. Here is the story.

The Markwells were moving; their books were in storage. Not the best time one would think to teach a child to read. But Mrs. Markwell was eager to let young John begin enjoying books, so she took the only material at hand – a liquor list – and began teaching him the sounds of the letters (a phonic approach to reading). The youngster was soon reading *vodka*, *rum*, *port* and the names of several other beverages.

John soon graduated from liquids and by the time he entered Grade 1 he had read about 250 books. Please note, Mrs. Markwell taught John *only* how to read during his preschool years; neither she nor her husband taught him any other academic matter. Furthermore, during John's

---

*name altered for privacy

school years she neither coached him nor provided incentives for good performance.

How *was* his performance? Pretty good.

In elementary school, John won more than a dozen silver cups for high achievement, and received the highest mark ever given for academic excellence. Later, in college, he was awarded the highest mark ever awarded for a graduation thesis in honors economics. Several universities – Yale, Northwestern, University of Toronto, of Pennsylvania, of Wisconsin, and of British Columbia – courted the boy with offers of scholarships and bursaries hoping to attract him for post-graduate studies.

An interesting detail of John's home education, aside from its brevity, was the fact that neither parent knew that early reading instruction was the principal method parents have used throughout history to raise their children's intelligence (the reason why reading instruction is featured at the Institute and in this book).

Take another case of startling intellectual advancement; one that admittedly provided a far greater challenge for the parent, Mrs. Green*, and for her son Peter as well.

Unlike John Markwell's mother, Peter's mother devoted every waking moment to her son's education. But there was a special need.

Peter's birth was exceedingly difficult. Mrs. Green went to the hospital at 7 PM with contractions occurring every three minutes. But the boy wasn't born until twenty-one hours later. During this long ordeal, pressure was apparently exerted on the infant's head for, when Peter was born, he had only a large dent where the back of his head should have been.

"Hideous!" the father cried, and refused to photo the baby.

At age two, Peter still lacked balance. He could neither crawl nor speak. Undaunted, Mrs. Green sat the infant on her knee, sang nursery rhymes and read to him for hours. Baby talk was never used. To develop Peter's pincer grip, she bought a set of Leggo – the smaller version to present a greater challenge and refine his grip. Then, to help him learn to control his leg muscles, she tied his feet to the pedals of a pedal cart and pushed him around. Next, seating the youngster on a tricycle Mrs. Green again pushed him, gradually reducing her pushing until, without the child knowing it, he was propelling himself.

By age four, Peter could still barely walk. His speech was so poor only his mother understood what he was attempting to say. Mrs. Green patiently taught him nursery rhymes and when, slowly, the boy did learn the rhymes, she coached him to enunciate every consonant distinctly. To

* name altered

crown her achievements, the mother began teaching Peter to read.

Because the family had now moved to a different neighborhood and no one knew of Peter's disability, Mrs. Green decided to enter him in Grade 1 and say nothing about his past. At that time the boy could read and write simple sentences and count to 100. The Grade 1 teacher promptly reported that Peter was brilliant. Indeed, he stood at or near the top of his class every year thereafter. In fact – and this is the clincher – when Peter completed Grade 4, the school principal recommended that Peter skip Grade 5 and enter Grade 6.

What irony! What tragedy – that Peter's classmates, whose brains had never been less than perfect, were doomed to face life with *under*developed brains because of parental neglect. Parents who, in all probability, provided the best of food and clothing they could afford for their children had, by omission, constricted their youngsters' intelligence to the unimpressive level of average.

And so, we have two surprises. Mrs. Markwell didn't intend to give her child genius intelligence, but did so. And Mrs. Green wanted only to normalize her brain-damaged child, but instead gave him a superior mind.

Think! If parents can give their children superior intelligence without meaning to, think what your chances of success are by using a tested program designed specifically to reach that goal.

What I am suggesting is not new. Knowledgeable parents of the past have raised their preschooler's intelligence to remarkable heights almost as a routine task – like dusting furniture and washing dishes. As might be expected, some parents worked more diligently at the venture than others and their offspring reveal the phenomenal range of human capability. Let's examine a few well-documented cases.

Jeremy Bentham

Jeremy Bentham, born in 1748, was educated to plan by his father, a lawyer. Jeremy was taught the alphabet even before he could speak (presumably indicating by gesture what letter was asked for). The child's early ability to read and write is seen in a letter to his grandmother:

> *Honoured Madam, I have been very much troubled with Sore Hands, but the Greatest Trouble was their preventing me thus long from writing to my dear Grand-Mama, indeed if you knew how bad they are still, you would be surprised at my handling my Pen at all, having only the use of my Thumb and Tip of my*

fore Finger, all the other Fingers of Each of my Hands being tied up together in a linnen Bag, otherwise I shod say a great deal more besides that I am Your Dutiful Grandson.

How old do you suppose young Jeremy was when he wrote this – ten, eight, six? He was three.

That same year the youngster read Rapin's *History of England* and, under his father's instruction, began studying Greek and Latin. He started school at age seven, entering the upper second form. At age ten, he passed the admission requirements for Oxford but the authorities wouldn't let him enter until he was twelve. Jeremy received his B.A. at fifteen and returned later to pick up his M.A. at eighteen. He became a philosopher, an economist, and a theoretical jurist who exerted great influence on the reforming thought of the nineteenth century.

John Stuart Mill

As an adult, Jeremy befriended James Mill who was twenty-five years his junior. James Mill shared Jeremy Bentham's belief that the value of school education was overrated, and that education at home was far superior. Like Bentham, Mill dismissed the notion that intelligence was genetically endowed, insisting that it was the result of early training. In his *Analysis of the Phenomena of the Human Mind*, Mill wrote,

> *Whoever has the power to regulate the sequence and the strength of the experiences which flow in upon a young mind, [will] decide the habits of association [that mind] will form, and to that extent [will] determine both the character and the ability of the later man.*

James Mill had the opportunity to test his belief in 1806 when his son John Stuart Mill was born. The only record we have of John Stuart Mill's early education is the description he wrote years later as an adult. He described it thus:

> *I have no remembrance of the time when I began to learn Greek, I have been told that it was when I was three years old. My earliest recollection on the subject is that of committing to memory what my father termed vocables, being lists of common Greek words with*

*their signification in English, which he wrote out for
me on cards.*

But we have an interesting omission here. To learn Greek by the
father's method, the three-year-old had to be able to read English. And
because he could not remember learning Greek, he must have learned to
read English even earlier in his pre-memory days – age two? Age one?

By age eight, John Stuart Mill's reading in Greek included:

> *a number of Greek prose authors, among whom I
> remember the whole of Herodotus, and of Xenophon's
> Cyropaedia and Memorials of Socrates; some of the
> lives of the philosophers by Diogenes Laertius; part of
> Lucian, and Isocrates ad Demonicum and Ad
> Nicoclem. I also read, in 1813 the first six dialogues
> (in the common arrangement) of Pluto, from
> Euthyphron to the Theoctetus inclusive.*

No Goldilocks and the three bears here!

Mill eventually became one of the most intellectually advanced
persons of all time, achieving fame as a philosopher, economist,
logician, and ethical theorist.

Karl Witte

For a warmer sort of early conditioning, we turn to the education of Karl
Witte, whose father, also called Karl, was the pastor in a German
village. Pastor Witte held strong and unorthodox views about education,
contending that what children learned before starting school would
dictate their lifelong achievement. He wrote:

> *Since children are essentially thinking animals, they
> are certain, from the moment they first use their own
> minds, to draw inferences and arrive at conclusions
> regarding everything they see, hear and touch; but if
> left to themselves will inevitably, because of their
> inability to form sound critical judgements, acquire
> wrong interests and thought habits which all the
> education of later life may not be able wholly to
> overcome.*

No sooner was the boy's umbilical cord snipped than the father began a full-time educational program that featured vocabulary growth. He reported:

> *Karl learned many things in the arms of his mother and in my own, such as one rarely thinks of imparting to children. He learned to know and name all the objects in the different rooms. The rooms themselves, the staircase, the yard, the garden, the stable, the well, the barn – everything from the greatest to the smallest, was frequently shown and clearly and plainly named to him, and he was encouraged to name the object as plainly as possible.*

When naming each item for the child, the parents pronounced the words loudly, clearly, slowly, and repeatedly. Baby talk was forbidden. The manner in which members of the household were organized to fill their role in the youngster's education suggests a dramatic performance:

> *We always spoke pure German, in other words, book German, in very simple and comprehensible – but none the less, choice – expressions, and always loudly, distinctly, and in an appropriately slow manner. We never allowed ourselves to make an improper use of intonation. We spoke as correctly, in every sense of the word, as we could. Obscure and intricate sentences and expressions, such as gave no distinct meaning, were scrupulously avoided.*

By age four, Karl was reading German. At age eight he was reading and speaking French, Italian, English, Latin, Greek, and had read – with enthusiasm! – Homer, Plutarch, Virgil, Cicero, Ossian, Fenelon, Florian, Metastasio, and Schiller. Young Karl entered the University of Leipzig at age nine, received his Ph.D. when he was thirteen, became Doctor of Laws and was appointed to the teaching staff of the University of Berlin as professor at age sixteen.

Heirs of the Witte Legacy

Pastor Witte described his son's education in the book *The Education of Karl Witte* which ran to more than a thousand pages. Every enterprising parent since that time has seemingly copied or borrowed from Witte's method, among them, James Thompson, of Belfast, father of the celebrated physicist, Lord Kelvin. Another, Adolf Berle, whose son, also called Adolf, became a child prodigy, passed the entrance examinations for Harvard at age twelve and began practicing law at nineteen. Adolf Jr. became a professor at Columbia Law School and a member of Franklin Roosevelt's brain trust.

Witte's book was translated into English by Leo Wiener, whose son Norbert – another child prodigy – entered Tufts College at age eleven and Harvard at fifteen. Norbert Wiener eventually became an eminent mathematician and founded the science of cybernetics.

The children, Bentham, Mill, Witte, Kelvin, Berle, and Wiener have been termed 'manufactured' geniuses. Their instruction at home was an intelligence-raising production. The children's brilliance was a studied matter, predicted, planned and sedulously pursued. Guesswork and chance were ruled out. Their achievements give us some idea of what the human mind is capable of.

Were the children gifted? Nonsense! Each parent stated emphatically they could achieve the same result with any normal child. Witte's father went so far as to publicize his exalted goal even before his son was born.

> *If God grants me a son, and if he, in your opinion, is not to be called stupid* [mentally deficient], *which Heaven forbid, I have long ago decided to educate him to be a superior man, without knowing in advance what his aptitudes may be.*

(As we will have already seen by Mrs. Green's performance, even being born mentally handicapped need not have barred the infant from achieving high intelligence.)

Similarly, Aaron Stern stated in his book *The Making of a Genius* that he intended to create a child with remarkable intelligence. Stern told visitors at the time of his daughter's birth that the infant before them was destined to become a genius by his instruction.

Did he succeed? Seems so. His daughter, Edith, became the youngest student ever to graduate from Florida Atlantic University. She began teaching mathematics at Washington State University at age fifteen.

As if this were not enough, Stern claimed he could achieve the same meteoric intelligence with children from a New Guinea stone-age culture (the Tasadays, discovered in 1971). He would increase the youngsters' intelligence well above that of average American children, he said, and do so in *six months*. The children would be reading by age two and would be able to begin public school by age three. Unfortunately, the Philippine government – protectorate of New

Guinea's minority tribes – refused to allow him guardianship of the infants, so the tantalizing experiment was thwarted.

Could Stern have made good his claim? Would the youngsters have dazzled skeptics, stunned critics, and left American parents gaping? It seems a long shot, but my money would have been on Stern.

So dizzying are the intellectual heights reached by past geniuses that it is hard to picture them as being free from the weaknesses the rest of us endure. John Stuart Mill sets our mind at rest with a modest description of himself and his shortcomings.

> *If I had been by nature extremely quick of apprehension, or had possessed a very accurate and retentive memory, or were of a remarkably active and energetic character, the trial would* [still] *not be conclusive; but in all these natural gifts I am rather below than above par; what I could do, could assuredly be done by any boy or girl of average capacity and healthy physical constitution: and if I have accomplished anything, I owe it, among other fortunate circumstances, to the fact that through the early training bestowed on me by my father, I started, I may fairly say, with an advantage of a quarter of a century over my contemporaries.*

As we have seen, intelligence can be raised – sometimes quite easily. Often overlooked, however, is the fact that intelligence can easily be lowered. Children enter the world with one-hundred-billion brain cells, quite enough to eventually match the performance of renowned thinkers throughout the ages: Leonardo da Vinci, Albert Einstein, Maria Curie and all the others whose names loom large in the hall of awe. Yet few fulfill their early promise. Why not?

The first obstacle – clearly demonstrated by Peter Green's classmates – is parental neglect: failing to recognize the importance of stimulating a child's early thought. Everything a child sees and hears will influence the way he or she thinks and acts. If a child is always with adults, he will pick up adult mannerisms. The quality of speech he hears in the home and the subjects discussed will boost his intelligence or not.

This point is so important it bears emphasis. *A child is learning every waking minute, not just while he is being formally taught.* Parental conversations with visitors and neighbors, the music played and the programs watched on television – all will influence the child's thinking.

But parents aren't the only source of instruction for a child, and this introduces a second powerful intelligence-reducing force; one we will call random ambient instruction.

When a child is old enough to mingle with other children, their thoughts and conversations – which usually reflect *their parents'* thoughts and conversations – will introduce an unsuspected and compelling form of instruction.

> *Everything seen and heard by a child will influence his or her thinking whether you want it to or not. A child's data-gathering brain is never turned off except when he or she is asleep.*

And so, as children grow, parental influence gradually competes with cultural and educational standards outside the home. Exposure to mediocrity (often electronically powered) and a generally impoverished use of language in everyday conversations are bound to influence children. Unless a child is intellectually challenged, many – if not most – of a child's one hundred billion brain cells will never be used. The eminent American psychologist and philosopher William James described the drab condition thus:

> *Compared to what we ought to be, we are only half-awake. We are making use of only a small part of our physical and mental resources. Stating the thing broadly, the human individual thus lives far within his limits. He possesses powers of various sorts which he habitually fails to use.*

This unflattering comment by a celebrated member of the American intelligentsia suggests that the person we see in the mirror each morning isn't long out of the trees. Public school education doesn't improve matters. Declining scholastic standards – constantly reported in the media – are an accepted part of life. Yet, educators are often the loudest in warning parents about the supposed dangers of preschool education – and particularly of reading instruction.

Low intelligence and ignorance are not qualities we should find acceptable, let alone rise to applaud (though this sometimes happens at school graduation ceremonies). By guarding your child from as many dumbing influences as you can, and stimulating his or her thought in ways to be described, you will assure him or her greater knowledge and enviable intelligence. But, we don't want brilliant misfits, so Chapter 18 helps you to equip your youngster with an ability to win friends easily.

10

What age of child will benefit from this program?

All ages. Even the unborn. Pre-natal conditioning is described in Chapter 2. Parents who have followed these practices report impressive results.

Instruction for infants up to age two follows a path well worn by the many parents who have given their children early superior intelligence. Older preschoolers will be able to speed ahead with more advanced methods. And if your child is already in school, he or she will benefit from the enriching procedures to be described.

Does the program work with every child?

Every child will benefit; however, the extent to which a child advances will depend on two matters: first, the child's age. A younger child – age two, three or four – is likely to be more receptive and responsive to parental guidance than an older child. Children age five or six would have to be judged individually. Teachers at the Institute find that even children who are age six or seven when they join the program advance dramatically once their learning difficulties have been sorted out. Special instruction is given in Chapter 15 for schoolchildren who are performing poorly.

A second contributor to success is how faithfully you pursue the program.

How bright is my child likely to become?

How bright would suit you? To a large extent, you set the limit. The goal of this book is modest enough: not entry to university by age twelve or thirteen, just a higher level of thinking than is common. And yet, despite the long, well-documented history of early intellectual stimulation there are some who question the safety of challenging a youngster's brain. To address this concern we should assess what intellectual load the human brain is capable of bearing.

We have seen the staggering accomplishments of Jeremy Bentham (IQ 180)* and John Stuart Mill (IQ 190)*. Though these figures are high they don't reveal the full power of the human brain when all the stops are pulled out. To get a clearer picture we must turn to William James Sidis.

William James *who*?

Genetic Studies of Genius, Volume II, Catherine M. Cox

Surprising, isn't it? – the person who represents a pinnacle of human intellectual power isn't even well known. Some background.

William James Sidis – called 'Willie' as a youngster – was named after his father's friend, the famous philosopher William James (mentioned earlier). The father, Boris Sidis, shared James' opinion that the limits of the mind were seldom reached. Boris Sidis set out to discover what the human brain was capable of, using Willie as a guinea pig.

If Willie's early education was extraordinary, his accomplishments were no less so. What did he accomplish? Hang on to your hat.

Willie began learning to spell before he was a year old. At eighteen months he was able to read *The New York Times*. When he learned how to use a children's encyclopedia, he became pretty much self-educating. At age three, as a surprise birthday gift for his father, the youngster taught himself Latin and read aloud from *Caesar's Gaulic Wars*. At four, Willie was typing letters to adult friends in excellent English or French. By then he was also fluent in Armenian, Russian, Turkish, Hebrew, Greek, and German.

At age six, after studying old calendars, Willie worked out a formula for determining on which day of the week any historical date fell (which he later patented). That same year Willie entered a Boston elementary school. He graduated seven months later. Working at home, Willie passed the entrance examinations for both the Harvard Medical School and the Massachusetts Institute of Technology before he entered high school where, though attending only two hours a day, he completed the four-year curriculum in six weeks. (He spent most of his time helping teachers mark math papers.)

After barring Willie twice because of his youth, Harvard finally admitted him at age eleven as a 'special student'. He was promptly invited to address the Harvard Mathematical Club on four-dimensional bodies, a subject too profound for many in the audience. At seventeen, he became a professor of mathematics at Rice University in Houston.

When Willie died in 1945, Abraham Sperling, then director of New York City's Aptitude Testing Institute reported,

> *In recent years, I have tested more than five thousand people. Of all the mentally superior individuals that I have seen, nobody begins to approach the intellect and perspicacity of William Sidis. According to my computations, he easily had an IQ between 250 and 300.*

This means that, in Sperling's opinion, William Sidis' intelligence approached almost twice that of Albert Einstein!

Was Willie brilliant because of his genes? Willie's parents maintained his meteoric intellect was due entirely to the exceptional training he had received – a message repeated over and over again by the parents of Bentham, Mill, Witte, Wiener, Kelvin, Berle, and Stern. Each genius-manufacturing parent has stated emphatically that their child was a very ordinary individual whose intelligence had been raised by training alone, and each parent confirmed they could achieve the same with any child – with *your* child, for example. If they could do it, so can you. However, our goal is far below the stellar intelligence of these high flyers. We are aiming for a mere IQ 140.

Smarts by Inheritance?

The Mega Society, an elite ultra-high IQ group having only 25 members world-wide, is an exclusive club for those with an IQ of at least 193. One member, Ferris Alger (IQ 197) abandoned by his father when the boy was a toddler, grew up in orphanages under harsh circumstances. He never secured a high school diploma. At age 17, the youth went in search of his unknown father and discovered, to his disappointment, that – in his own words – "He didn't have any brains".

What do these accomplishments say about the nature-nurture argument and the importance of genes? They say that when we are discussing intelligence, we should forget about genes. Doubtless each of us has a genetically predetermined top intellectual limit (which each of us fails to reach). So, any argument about who, or what race, is intellectually superior is futile. To illustrate, you may have the genetic ability to achieve an IQ of 300 whereas my genes wouldn't permit me to score much higher than 275. But neither of us approaches anywhere near these upper levels, so how can we say which of us is inherently brighter? Moreover, there is a danger in attributing children's intelligence to genes. Parents are then led to believe their child's intelligence has already been fixed, so why bother trying to increase it?

Inheriting a genetically superior brain is not enough. Early instruction alone will determine what advantage has been secured by inheriting a more powerful thinking organ. The stunning discoveries made of brain development (described in Chapter 17) by researchers at the University of California, Berkeley, vaporize the myth of intellectual superiority through genes. David Krech, a member of the team concluded, "We can now undo the effects of generations of breeding.

Heredity is not enough. All the advantages of inheriting a good brain can be lost if you don't have the right psychological environment in which to develop it."

We now see clearly that you, the parent, are the one who establishes your child's upper intellectual limit, so *you* are obviously the best person to answer the question, 'How bright is my child likely to become?' What is your answer? What level will you settle for? To give your child an IQ of 200 would require a great deal of work even if it were advisable. Similarly IQ 180 might require more than the convenience education presented in this book. IQ 160 is achievable, and an IQ of 140 – the threshold of genius – is easily reached. In fact, IQ 140 is the lowest level we expect a child to reach at the Institute, bearing in mind that many of our children attend only a few mornings or afternoons each week. You, on the other hand, have all day with your youngster. Or do you? Some parents must return promptly to full-time jobs. This means a child may spend his or her day at a daycare center or with a sitter. And yet, even single-parents have overcome this handicap and raised children of remarkable intelligence by the methods to be presented.

The purpose of this chapter has been to show you, first, the astonishing power of the human brain, and second, the ease with which your child can gain exceptionally high intelligence. A reasonably accurate way to estimate your child's advancing IQ is dealt with in Appendix 2.

Your three-year-old may not be able to write the equivalent of, *Dear Grandma, am having a great time here at Disney World. Wish you were here so I could take you on the roller coaster*, as a contemporary Jeremy Bentham might, nor devour the Encyclopedia Britannica as John Stuart Mill might, but he or she is capable of astonishing brilliance. Would it not be a modest and reasonable goal for you to raise your child's intelligence by just forty IQ points? What a difference it will make to his or her future!

Again, the important points:

    1 – Raising children's intelligence is easy.

    2 – You need no experience to raise your child's intelligence to a genius level.

    3 – The knowledge and abilities your child acquires before starting school will greatly influence his or her success all through life.

The Emperor's Trump

As a boy, Napoleon Bonaparte was so clumsy he couldn't throw a stone in the right direction. He was not only a poor marksman, he never learned to ride well. Described as being more than awkward – in many ways helpless – Napoleon was unable to arrange his hair in pigtails and side curls as was then the fashion. *But brains!* Ah yes.

2

Prebirth

You may already have a child. If so, the information presented here could be arriving a little late. But mothers generally bear more than one child, so whatever we discuss could make future pregnancies less mystifying and more fascinating. Also, you may gain a better understanding of some characteristics your present child displays, or might yet display.

Our concern here is with options that are available to pregnant women, and even to women before they become pregnant. Dealing with matters at a seminal level we are obliged to consider the Repository for Germinal Choice, at Escondido, California. Administrators at the Repository presume to guarantee high intelligence for children by genetic means: a concept that runs contrary to the beliefs stated in Chapter 1. We must therefore address the matter.

First, some background.

The Repository was opened in 1980 by millionaire Robert Graham to store and distribute the sperm of Nobel Prize winners (later, however, non-Nobel sperm became acceptable, though donors still had to have a high IQ – between 130 to 185). The Repository provided free vials of high quality frozen sperm to any woman wishing to become pregnant provided the woman could supply proof of high intelligence. The sperm, donated by brilliant scientists, was thought to guarantee brilliant offspring.

Here was the plan. At the appropriate moment in the woman's menstrual cycle, her doctor or obstetrician would thaw the Nobel Prize winner's sperm and insert it. Voila! Another genius on the way.

Unfortunately, founder Graham overlooked an important point: if winning a Nobel Prize was the product of quality genes, then it was the *parents* of the Nobel Prize winners – not the winners themselves – who possessed the intellectually powerful genetic mix. But even then, the single sperm that chanced to germinate the egg within the Nobel Prize winner's mother was only one of 300 to 500 million completely different sperm cells in the father's ejaculate, each sperm cell of which could create an entirely different individual with different features and capabilities.

Clearly, in attempting to establish a link between special sperm cells and bright progeny, we would have astronomically high odds working against securing a 'winning' combination. Why then do the recipients of frozen sperm report such excellent results? Ah yes, we will return to this detail later.

Now, back to the womb. Lest we forget our humble beginnings, a review might be appropriate. You, I, and everyone else on the planet started out as an egg about the size of the period at the end of this sentence. In due course, a microscopic sperm cell penetrated the egg and triggered the creative process that eventually formed an embryo; one that, strangely, was indistinguishable from that of a cow, a monkey, a lizard, or even a bird. Then we developed a tail and gill pouches. Fortunately, programmed cell suicide terminated our luck in that direction and switched production to the creation of bone and muscle. About the twenty-second day of development, our heart began to beat. Unfortunately, it was situated at the front of our head. But matters improved, and at the end of four weeks the heart was tucked into our chest. We then went through a continued bone-destroying, bone-making procedure to accommodate our growing embryo. By day 56, we no longer answered to 'embryo'; we became a fetus.

During development – yours, mine, and everybody else's – our fetus was vulnerable to various upsets, each of which had the potential to cause long-term damage. Life in the womb, we are told, is perilous – especially during the first three months (the first trimester) – and whatever steps can be taken to assure health and tranquility must be observed. Though we can't control the genes that build a fetus, we can at least help assure its peace and contentment. And most surprising of all, it is thought that we can educate the fetus.

Education is said to begin in the womb whether mothers realize it or not. In fact, specialists in prenatal matters tell us that what we experience in the womb will influence our eventual nature as powerfully as our genes. Waiting until a child is born to begin its education is likened to starting a ball game with the batter already at first base. North Americans were awakened to the apparent marvels of prenatal education when retired firefighter, Joseph Susedik, and his Japanese wife, Jitsuko, revealed they had educated their four daughters before they were born. Beginning at the fifth month of pregnancy, Jitsuko taught each fetus the numbers and the alphabet – a performance sure to provoke smiles if not laughter from neighbors. But the laughter must have faded when, after birth, the children's spectacular achievements became known. By the time their controversial home education program hit the news, the Susedik's five-year-old was reading at a Grade 5 level. Her sister, age seven, was entering Grade 7. Their nine-year-old was entering Grade 8. And the eldest, at twelve, was a pre-med student in her second year of university.

Critics of the mother's in-womb educational program attributed the children's accomplishments to intense parental interest and involvement after each child was born. (In passing, I must mention that teachers at the Ledson Institute achieve equally spectacular early intellectual advancement by post-birth influence alone. See Appendix 1.) In any case, we will soon see that a fetus is receptive to everything it hears.

In the past, little was known about fetal life. But today, prenatal psychologists with their greater knowledge and advanced technology can tell us volumes about the unborn child: its health, its happiness, and its growth. And, as we will see, health, happiness, and growth play important roles in determining – even dictating – the quality of life a child will experience after birth.

Quietness usually reigns in the womb for the first six or seven weeks of pregnancy. Then, about the eighth week, activity picks up. The fetus is able to move its head, arms, and trunk easily and can express its likes and dislikes by jerking and kicking, though these movements are too feeble for the mother to feel. With the arrival of 3D ultrasound, researchers have been able to observe a fetus 'walking' and yawning at the end of the third month and, a month later, frowning, squinting, and grimacing.

Sometime between the fourth and fifth month, the mother notices a poking or kicking in her belly – the so-called moment of quickening – as the fetus responds to sound and melody. The mother's voice, especially her singing, contributes greatly to fetal contentment. Moreover, the fetus shows well-defined preferences in music. Vivaldi and Mozart rate among the top ten. Brahms and Beethoven, alas, tie with rock music in upsetting the fetus. (Imagine the unpleasantness a fetus may experience when rock music is played at its usual loudness.) The unborn child kicks violently (though not in tempo) when objectionable music is played. Some mothers have been obliged to stop attending concerts because their unborn children reacted so stormily to the music.

Cases have been reported of adults who demonstrated an uncanny knowledge of, or fascination with, certain musical pieces, only to learn later from their mothers that the same music had been played while they occupied the womb.

If you are pregnant, remember, when you speak, someone is listening through the wall – through the wall of your stomach, that is.

The fetus hears clearly beginning about the sixth month. This doesn't mean you should begin whispering. Not at all. The sound and idiosyncratic rhythm of your voice have a singularly soothing effect on the fetus – a pacifying influence that will continue to work its magic even after the child is born.

Between six and seven months, the fetus is able to scratch, cry, hiccup, and most surprising of all, smile. Consciousness, or awareness, begins at this time. Neural circuits in the fetal brain are now as highly developed as those of a newborn. A week or two later, the child's brain waves become sufficiently distinct for us to know whether he or she is awake or asleep.

Under the influence of either medication or hypnosis, adults have regressed to a fetal state and disclosed matters that were later confirmed to be true by their astonished mothers. Psychiatrist Stanislav Grof tells of a patient who, when regressed, described noises he could hear outside the womb: laughter, yelling and the blare of trumpets. He then announced he was about to be born. On contacting his patient's mother, Dr. Grof learned that the excitement of a carnival had in fact induced his patient's birth. The amazed mother said she had kept the information secret because her own mother had warned her about the possibility of an inconvenient birth if she attended the carnival.

In another case, a group of patients under hypnosis were asked to describe the position of their head and shoulders at the moment of birth. Their descriptions were found to match the description of their births that had been locked away in the obstetrician's office for twenty years.

Why are birth memories seldom remembered without resort to drugs or hypnosis? Apparently, the hormone oxytocin, produced in the mother's brain to induce uterine contractions and lactation, induces forgetfulness. As proof, when the drug is injected into laboratory animals, they suffer amnesia.

Everyone knows that a pregnant woman eats for two. The food she eats contributes to her own health as well as to her unborn child. The mother's nutritional intake is therefore of major importance. With the wealth of processed foods readily available today, we might study it and assess its value.

Nutrition is not the first concern of those who manufacture or process foods. Their main interest lies in taste, appearance, texture, cost of production, and whether the consumer will purchase the food again. Fine, but because nutritional value must take priority over every other attribute of foods the pregnant mother would wisely avoid any nutritional gamble and prepare her own meals. 'Fast foods' – hamburgers, chips, pizzas, doughnuts, salt-drenched edibles high in saturated, hydrogenated and trans fats – are not the foodstuffs of champions. Each sugary junk food or drink (termed 'canned candy') the mother swallows, every medication or pill she consumes – even aspirin – influences the health and comfort of the fetus.

Antidepressant drugs require mention because they present a special danger to the fetus. Antidepressants are designed for, and tested by, adults. When prescribed for children, the principal ingredient in antidepressants, serotonin, increases the already super-rich amount of this chemical normally present in children's brains. In high doses, serotonin has been seen to alter the anatomy of children's brains and, by a quirk called conversion, to double the likelihood of suicidal thought. What comparable effect the drug, taken by the mother, might have on the embryo isn't known, but if a pregnant woman feels the need for mood enhancement, renting a comedy video might be safer.

Then, there's nicotine.

The fetal heartbeat has been seen to quicken not merely when a mother lights a cigarette but – and this is astonishing – when the mother even *thinks* of lighting a cigarette. Such was the almost incredible finding of Dr. Michael Lieberman described in the American Journal of Obstetrics (Aug. 5. '70). Think of it! The mother didn't even have to touch the unlit cigarette to her lips to upset the fetus. How is this possible?

The fetus and mother are physically, psychically, and emotionally, linked. They are truly one. Anything that influences the mother is seen to generate a response in the fetus. Experiments with a group of chemicals called catecholamines – found in the blood of animals and humans when they are fearful – revealed that placid animals, when injected with the chemical, quickly became terrified. Knowing the alteration in mood that chemicals can produce, we should not be surprised to learn that every human mood and emotion generates its own unique chemical mix. It is this emotion-generating soup – fluctuating for better or worse with the mother's mood – that she transmits to her fetus.

But why is nicotine so dangerous to the unborn child?

Smoking lowers the oxygen in the mother's blood. Though the circulation system of the fetus is independent from the mother's, the fetus apparently senses the onset of a disagreeable condition. In other words, the fetus receives advance notice – chemically triggered – of an impending threat to its contentment.

With abundant proof confirming the harmful effects of smoking on the fetus, continued smoking by a pregnant woman is not merely inconsiderate, it is virtually criminal.

Though the perils of smoking are well known, the perils of alcohol are not. Yet alcohol presents far graver danger to the fetus. Alcohol passes through the placenta as easily as the normal life-sustaining fluids. Investigators tell us that the more alcohol a woman drinks the more likely will her fetus – and eventual child – fall victim to fetal alcohol syndrome. Some of its tragic symptoms are mental retardation, hyperactivity, heart murmur and facial deformity. The bottom line is still worse: heavy drinking can not only deform the fetus, it can kill the child.

A final concern: caffeine. Investigators at the University of Washington found a correlation between caffeine (whether it is in coffee, cola, tea or cocoa) and some birth disorders. Those in the study who consumed the most caffeine had babies with the highest rate of poor muscle tone and low activity levels. Though more study is needed to confirm the caffeine-induced afflictions, a wise move would be to avoid caffeine or at least reduce its consumption.

In studying 2000 women throughout pregnancy and birth, Dr. Monika Lukech, psychologist at Constantine University, Frankfurt, concluded that the mother's attitude was the greatest single influence in determining a child's nature. The next greatest influence was the quality of the mothers' relationship with her husband or partner. The environment, too, was seen to play an important role. Obviously, an easy, trouble-free life helps keep both mother and fetus happy. But even when the mother is burdened with external stresses – social, environmental, or financial – the contentment of the fetus will be profoundly influenced by the way the mother feels about the unborn child.

Take comfort in knowing that occasional negative emotions or distressing events are not going to damage your child permanently. Pat your enlarged stomach and say, "It doesn't matter what the world throws at me. At least I've got you. You and me, we're going to do all right." Your child will revel in the warmth of that thought, moreover, your relaxed manner will help assure a painless delivery when that grand moment arrives.

If a mother fears the impending birth, she might be aided by hypnosis. Fortified by hypnotically induced positive thoughts, mothers are then less reliant on unnatural birth aids. These include various drugs that eighty percent of women are given, the use of forceps in thirty percent of all vaginal births (a practice that can inflict lasting injury on the emerging child), and Caesarian section employed in fifteen percent of all deliveries (and condemned by many obstetricians).

Childbirth has become a highly profitable male dominated industry. To have a baby without the services of an obstetrician or gynecologist is thought to be almost as impudent as trying to get on the merry-go-round without a ticket. But birth is better and safer, we are told, without

21

mechanical manipulation or surgery. Moreover, evidence suggests that babies miss an important experience and sensation when they arrive other than through the birth canal. Pregnant women would be wise to read *The American Way of Birth*, by Jessica Mitford.

Who will deliver your child – an obstetrician, a doctor, a midwife? Midwives are thought to be more sympathetic to mothers and more likely to view childbirth as a natural biological process. Medical men, on the other hand, sometimes see childbirth as a pathogenic state.

Having been obliged by circumstance to deliver a child myself, I might offer a word of guidance to fathers caught in a similar frenzied situation. There is no need to immediately cut the umbilical cord. I didn't learn this until later, so, not having a knife handy, I severed the cord with my teeth – which isn't too different from chewing through the rubber hose connected to your showerhead.

Now, to tidy up a deferred matter. Why did the mothers who received the highly touted Nobel sperm report such excellent results?

Why indeed! Because their progeny enjoyed red-carpet treatment all the way. In the first place, not just anyone could get the sperm. The recipient had to prove she had high intelligence. Membership in Mensa helped. Next, the recipient had to be married, thus increasing the likelihood of an emotionally and financial stable home environment. But the key requirement – and here we might sound the trumpets – was that the mother had to be willing to provide an exceptionally good education for the child (showing proof, of course, that she had enough money to provide that education).

As if these ideal requirements were not enough, recipients then provided – without being asked – the most powerful contributor of all: high expectation. The children were expected to be bright. Parents watched eagerly for signs of cleverness to support their expectations. "Hey, Hank, Franklin just fell on the carpet. See where his head landed? Right beside the encyclopedia. We've got a real winner here!"

What can you learn from all this? Expect great things of your child. Chat over with your fetus what you would like him to achieve, or just tell him that whatever goal he chooses, you will love him – or her – all the same.

Mensa

Mensa is an international organization for those with IQs of 135 or higher. Critics of Mensa point out that qualification for membership rests wholly on the ability to solve problems that can be presented on paper, and members might be intellectually unspectacular in other ways.

3

The Newborn

The apocryphal tale of a pregnant woman dropping her plough, delivering her baby, picking up the plough and plodding home to the shack, if true, remains a tribute to courageous women of the past. And yet, even today, the task of earning a living while bearing and raising children can be daunting. How long will the new mother be able to spend at home with her baby? Is she on maternity leave? Are there others who could look after the infant while the mother returns to work? Whatever the situation, the person who ends up looking after the child should have access to the information presented here, and we must leave the matter at that.

After birth, the baby and mother should be permitted to enjoy their combined triumph. Yet, regrettably, the pair are often immediately separated. One might call this a barbaric practice but I don't think barbarians would impose isolation on a newborn infant. According to reports concerning child-parent bonding, the first need of the mother and infant is not food or sleep, but body contact with each other. Mother and newborn need to look at each other, and to touch. The infant needs to hear clearly the familiar voice he heard muffled for so long. Unfortunately, these precious moments of togetherness are lost if the mother has been drugged. Worse, because the powers of bonding between mother and infant are greatest immediately after birth, delay in bonding can jeopardize their relationship.

Language

The sounds of speech are not new to the newborn. The embryo has heard conversations through the stomach wall for months, though the words were muffled. However, we may assume that the rhythms and cadence of a specific language (the mother tongue) have been securely fixed in the child's mind before he sees daylight.

Up to the age of three months, infants chatter more frequently when they are spoken to. On hearing the mother's voice the baby will usually smile and 'talk back' with small bursts of liquid sound. Still, the newborn infant presents a puzzle for parents. Yes, the inept butterball lying before them has heard words, but could the words mean anything? We too easily assume that a child's thinking is as inept as his overall muscular ability when, in fact, the muscular challenge facing the baby is no different from that of an adult who is called upon to operate a complicated machine for the first time without instruction.

The task of learning to manipulate the appropriate muscles – this one or that one, or a combination of several – to achieve a specific movement requires diligence, thought, and concentration – which may explain why mentally deficient children usually lack grace of movement. But the infant's physical clumsiness doesn't certify intellectual clumsiness. We but roughly understand the workings of a young brain and its scope. Though your child may not be able to chat until he reaches age two or later, he will be able to understand words long before he gains control of the appropriate speech muscles to produce those words himself.

Aaron Stern, who followed the vocabulary-building procedure described by Karl Witte, records in his book *The Making of a Genius* that his daughter Edith could identify, by gesture, 400 spoken words when she was five months old. Furthermore, Stern claimed that any child could accomplish the same if appropriately trained. The Susedik children, mentioned in Chapter 2, achieved even more impressive early speech skill. Their parents reported the children could say "Mama" and "Papa" at three weeks of age: an astonishing achievement attributed by the father and mother to the fact they spoke constantly to each child while it tenanted the womb.

Children's brains are sometimes likened to sponges, quick to absorb any information that comes their way. Whether children's brains are any spongier than yours or mine is questionable. But one thing is certain. Being free of the myriad adult concerns – earning a living; dealing with social matters; car, house, and health problems; mortgage and taxes – children's minds are able to concentrate more fully on any matter presented to them. For this reason, parents would wisely seize the brief dominion they have over their child's education. As children grow they will meet new sources of learning, but until children reach the age of two or three, parents rule their child's education. During this short period – a time of imprinting – parents will establish preferences and leanings in their child's attitude and conduct, and parents will do this whether they intend to or not. In other words, to neglect an infant's education doesn't mean the infant will stop learning. It means, instead, that the child's education will become haphazard or random – the situation Pastor Witte warned of when he said:

> *Since children are essentially thinking animals, they are certain, from the moment they first use their own minds, to draw inferences and arrive at conclusions regarding everything they see, hear and touch; but if left to themselves will inevitably, because of their inability to form sound critical judgements, acquire wrong interest and thought habits which all the education of later life may not be able wholly to overcome.*

Your child may not become a university professor at age sixteen as Witte's son did, but whatever goal he eventually settles on will be more easily reached if you enrich his early thought. The Pastor's words are clear: control your child's early thinking lest chance and accident handle the task in a possibly unproductive or displeasing way.

Parents usually look forward to the day they can begin teaching their child when, in fact, the dribbling pupil sits before them waiting to be taught. How to start? Though we know the spectacular intellectual accomplishments of past manufactured geniuses, the early procedures their parents used to secure this brilliance are vague. Pastor Witte alone gave details on how he conducted his son's education. His simple method is easily copied. Begin, as Pastor Witte did – and as Aaron Stern did when educating his daughter Edith – by building your child's *listening* vocabulary.

The procedure is simple. Carry your infant around the home and name each item: *door, window, curtains, sofa, chair, table, bowl, broom,* and *sink.* The exercise is so simple it could become boring when you have repeated it a few times. But it won't be boring for your pupil, and, more importantly, repetition will speed learning.

Read children's books to your child. He or she may not understand the words, but that isn't important. Your voice is the sweetest, most reassuring sound your child knows. Sit the youngster on your lap so he can see the text and pictures while you read. Several benefits are gained by reading to a child. First, reading stories aloud permits you to talk to your child without having to invent conversation. Second, reading provides moments of warm physical contact with the child. Third, books become, in this way, pleasantly associated with parental attention and affection. And lastly, the child may detect a relationship between your spoken words and the lines of small black squiggles on the page: a connection that will be made clearer if you run your finger along beneath the words as you read. (This will also condition the youngster to the rule of left-to-right reading – sometimes a stumbling block when children begin learning to read.)

The books you read to your child at this time will probably become the first books he reads himself, so select the books carefully. (Suggested reading materials are described in Chapter 8.) The print should be large with plenty of space between the lines. Avoid books with wolves, witches or other frightening villains. Though a child might be able to tolerate these grim characters while perched safely on your lap, he won't want to encounter them when he begins to read on his own.

Read stories and magazine articles aloud for your child. Read aloud the flyers, handbills, folders and the too-good-to-be-missed offers that fill your mailbox, and voice your comments on them. Talk about the neighbors, the seasons, your plans and hopes – any topic you choose. Tell your child the story of your life and the events that led to the youngster's birth. Your voice will not only expand your child's listening vocabulary, it will generate warmth and togetherness: a continuation of the bonding initiated in the womb.

If your child must be placed in a seat while you move around the home, chatting becomes all the more important because talking is a sort of touch beyond reach. Sing to the child occasionally. If you don't know the words to a song, "la-la-la" will do nicely. Talk or sing to the infant while you feed him, burp him, bath him, and change his diapers.

The most difficult word your child learns to recognize is the *first* one. Each word after that is easier. To understand his or her first word a child must recognize that there is a relationship between a voiced sound and an object. Learning the first word can be made simple or difficult by the way the word is taught.

Begin by introducing your baby to the names of objects he sees daily. The child's bath could serve as a good starting point. Say *bath* several times just before placing the infant in the water, and again several times while he is in it. Eventually, the child will associate the sound of the word *bath* with the pleasant experience of warm water, and he will show, by his enthusiasm, and perhaps by a glance at the bath, that he knows the word has some connection with bathing.

When teaching the child to recognize a word, don't obscure its sound by burying the word among other words: "Would Marigold like her bath now?" or "Isn't it nice to have a bath?" Neither of these word-groups conveys the sound of *bath*. The child would have to be a wizard to isolate the sound of *bath* amid the jumble of other sounds. Similarly, don't teach "Stockwell's hat" or "That's a ball", just teach *hat* and *ball*.

Continue with the names of other objects the child sees frequently: *diaper*, *spoon*, *sponge*, *powder*, and so on. Once a child begins to show response to spoken words (don't expect this to happen overnight) you will be able to enlarge his vocabulary easily if you observe a few simple rules.

1. Voice each word slowly, clearly, and loudly, while attracting the child's attention to the object with your hand or while holding the object in your hand. Repeat the procedure a few times each day.

2. Teach your child only nouns, that is to say, the names of things you can see; for example, *hot* and *cold* aren't nouns, they're adjectives and you can't see them. Other parts of speech can be taught later when the child begins to form sentences.

3. Add new words one at a time, but only when the child can easily identify all the preceding words. Remember, nothing slows learning as surely as confusion (for adults and babies alike).

4. Avoid teaching, close together in time, objects of similar size or similar shape, or words having similar sounds; for example, *dog* and *doll*, or *doll* and *wall*.

5. Avoid teaching, close together in time, items situated near each other or objects that are part of – or might be considered part of – some other item; for example, after teaching *hand*, let time elapse before teaching *fingers*. Similarly, let time elapse between teaching *wall* and *window*, the latter being, properly, a part of the wall.

6. Teach the names of only those objects the youngster sees often, objects that form part of the child's daily life.

7. Keep a list of the words you teach and review them often.

◆ ◆ ◆

The newborn child sleeps a lot; this, a continuation of prenatal life. The newborn tends to follow the sleep pattern established by the mother during the preceding months. From this, we see that what happens after birth is really a continuation of life in the womb. But now, having moved from the 'inner classroom' to the 'outer classroom', education accelerates.

The first condition for early learning isn't intellectual stimulation but the absence of problems. Fretting, unhappy babies can't think about anything other than what is bothering them. If education is to hold their interest, babies have to be healthy and contented. Keeping babies healthy is the subject for a book in itself; one matter, though, is of sufficient importance to beg attention here: food.

Nutrition

Breastfeeding would hardly require mentioning except for an uncertainty about its value, and because a wrong decision by the mother could inflict long-term harm to her baby. Should new mothers breast-feed their infant or not? This puzzler is best answered by the mother. But before she answers, the mother would be wise to assess her ability to produce quality milk.

Traditionally, almost all new mothers breastfed their infants. But at that earlier time, sodium-saturated potato chips, popcorn, and TV snacks were not popular foodstuffs. Nor were sugar-laden drinks, artificial sweeteners, foods rich in saturated or manufactured fats, or those having fillers, emulsifiers, and various colorings that one-or-another authority considers injurious to health. From the baby's standpoint, it's a wild game out there. And the fact that college graduates are reportedly four times more likely to breastfeed than others is small consolation to the youngster busy on the nipple.

Considering that everything the mother eats will be passed on to the infant, scrutiny of everything the mother ingests becomes mandatory. But food and drink are not the only concern. Almost every chemical that enters the mother's body can pass into her milk. This includes sedatives, tranquilizers, decongestants, antibiotics, laxatives, caffeine, antihistamines and contraceptive pills. The nagging truth is that we don't know the extent of damage that any one chemical can cause. Chemicals that *might* be harmful to an adult can, more perniciously, dwarf a child's mental or physical growth. Children are much more vulnerable than adults because they are growing – a danger constantly repeated in medical literature.

When you consider the various ways mother's milk can be adulterated and the possible annoyance the mother may endure by sore or cracked nipples and the potentially embarrassing need to feed the child in a social setting, cow's milk served in a bottle seems a wiser choice. At least we know the cow has pursued a reasonably healthful time-tested diet free from the contaminants that plague our human diet. By assuring your youngster a healthy diet, you will have a potentially good pupil for the program to be described. But good food and good health aren't enough to guarantee a baby's contentment, and without a happy pupil, education can be both difficult and slow. Let's consider a few other matters that help assure an infant's happiness.

Womb Music

Because babies sleep most of the time, parents should make sure their child's sleep is peaceful. Babies sometimes cry even when placed in what would be for adults an ideal sleep-inducing situation: a dark, quiet room. Why? One reason is that newborn infants have never experienced quiet before. During their long occupancy of the womb, babies were accustomed to the sounds *heard* by the mother and sounds *made* by the mother. Even when the pregnant mother experienced quiet, babies continued to hear the mother's intestinal activity and her heartbeat. Not surprisingly, the sound of a heartbeat has been found to soothe children even after they are born.

Dr. Hajime Murooka, professor of gynecology at the Nippon Medical University, Tokyo, discovered that of 403 infants who stopped crying after hearing the amplified sound of a human heartbeat, 161 went to sleep in an average of forty-one seconds.

In another study the sound of a human heartbeat was piped into a nursery filled with newborn babies. The result was surprising. The sound not only pacified infants, they ate more, weighed more, slept more, breathed better, cried less and were less likely to be sick.

A ticking clock has long been thought to calm a restive child. However, Dr. Murooka found the ticking of a metronome to be ineffective. And holding an infant close to the mother's heart turned out to be only 40 percent effective in comparison with 84 percent effectiveness of an amplified heart beat. Dr. Murooka subsequently produced a recording entitled *Lullaby from the Womb*. The recording presents the sound of a human heartbeat as heard in the uterus of a woman eight months pregnant. It quiets infants as if by magic.

The old-fashioned rocking cradle has long been known to pacify a fretful infant. But only recently has an acceptable reason been offered for its influence. The gentle rocking motion is thought to soothe a baby because it approximates the semi-weightless movement the youngster enjoyed for so long in the amniotic fluid of the womb. A rocking cradle is, therefore, a better choice of bed for your infant than a crib, particularly during the infant's first few months of life.

When the baby is awake, a pacifier or dummy nipple is often useful for keeping him in good spirits. Dentists report that pacifiers will not endanger the correct formation of teeth.

TLC

An important condition for the baby's contentment is, of course, plenty of tender loving care. Parents hardly need coaching in this, but how often and how quickly should parents respond to a child's cry? Is there any risk of spoiling a child by being too responsive? A study conducted at Johns Hopkins University showed that prompt response to an infant's cry helped to form a stronger bond between parent and child. Moreover, researchers claim that a child will not be spoiled during the first seven months of life no matter how promptly or repeatedly parents respond to its call. Letting a baby 'cry it out' is seen to be neither desirable nor beneficial.

But wait! Why should a child have to cry out in the first place? Awake or sleeping, a child should be near its mother. When placed in a body sling, babies enjoy body contact with the mother – togetherness – while freeing her to pursue other activities. During moments when a baby seat or crib is a more suitable resting-place, the seat should be placed so the baby can see the mother.

Vision

Once a child's contentment has been secured – or at least made more likely – we can promote learning by enriching the child's field of vision. There are, of course, limitations to what is possible. A newborn baby has 20/500 vision – extreme near-sightedness. The child is able to see objects only if they are close. He can make out the features of the mother's face eight inches away, but hasn't the visual accommodation necessary to see a tree fifty yards away.

Though babies can't see objects clearly that are outside the crib, this doesn't justify obstructing the child's view. Indeed, visual deprivation can disadvantage infants. In a study conducted at the Gesellschaft für Rationelle Psychologie, in Munich, thirty-eight children were raised in special Plexiglas cribs that permitted unobstructed viewing in all direction. The children were seen to demonstrate remarkably quick mental development when compared with other children who had been raised in conventional cribs. Obviously, where safety permits, high sides on the infant's bed and travel conveyances should be avoided. If your child's crib or cradle has bars that require padding to protect the baby's head, wrap each bar individually with padding instead of surrounding the cradle with a high protective mat.

By studying infant eye movement with television monitoring cameras, researchers are able to determine how carefully babies can track objects and focus on them. But this doesn't tell us the range of objects that are merely perceived. For example, when you focus on an object, various other items are perceived in the periphery of your vision. And so, though an infant's focused vision is limited in scope, the child isn't blind to other things. They are merely seen less clearly. For some activities even this unfocused vision is adequate. Mobiles can help.

Mobiles

A mobile, as the name implies, is something that moves. Almost anything suspended by string from the ceiling might serve as a mobile: a Christmas decoration, a soup ladle, even an empty detergent container. Turning slowly, as suspended objects will, such mobiles can provide your baby with a continually fascinating center of interest. During the first few months, when lying on their backs, babies tend to face one way or the other. Position a mobile in the direction your child's head is turned most of the time. If he has two favorite positions, hang a second mobile in that direction.

A better type of mobile is one to which you can attach decorations. An empty facial-tissue box can be decorated, each side differently, with pieces of foil, wrapping paper, pictures or patterns cut from magazines, bottle tops, buttons, ribbons, or almost anything colorful. Keep the mobile bright. If your pictures show real objects – and a large front view of a human face is recommended – make sure the baby will see it right-way-up in his side-reclining position. If you construct several such mobiles, you will be able to change them every few days. Variety will increase your child's interest. If you have an aquarium, position it beside the crib at the baby's eye level. The fish will provide a constantly changing spectacle. If you haven't an aquarium, you might suspend goldfish in a clear plastic bag of water over the side of the crib.

Infant Mobility

The baby itself should be kept mobile. Babies need to be handled and moved about frequently. Our civilization is unique in the amount of physical separation it imposes on infants. Carriages, cribs, baby chairs and bouncers make it all too easy for the mother to detach herself from the child.

A baby's best form of transportation is a baby sling. The infant, positioned at the front (almost back at home plate, as it were), enjoys the best of all possible worlds. The baby will delight in the warmth and movement of your body: a condition he or she enjoyed so contentedly before birth. If a sling is impractical because of the tasks to be attended, a semi-reclining baby seat – one with a head support – will permit him or her to accompany you on your round of household duties.

A child in frequent motion sees a moving world. This too has been found to influence brain growth. Professor Boris Klosovskii, chief of neurosurgery at the Academy of Medical Sciences of the [former]

U.S.S.R. conducted an unusual experiment in movement with newborn puppies and kittens. One group of animals – the control group – was kept in a confined area. The second group of animals – the experimental group – was similarly confined but their enclosure was mounted on a slowly rotating turntable. This latter group saw, in consequence, a constantly moving world. Beginning on the tenth day of the experiment (and ending on the nineteenth day), Professor Klosovskii began sacrificing the animals in pairs – one control animal and one experimental animal – to note any difference in brain growth. The brain cells in the experimental animals (those that had been slowly rotated) were found to be from 22.8 to 35 percent larger and more mature than those of the control group. Frequent movement is therefore seen to exert a surprisingly beneficial influence on children's intelligence. But, please note, the professor didn't plunk his animals in front of a TV set. No experiment has shown that a small two-dimensional *representation* of movement – as a TV screen provides – stimulates brain growth (though a shrinking effect would not be surprising).

Crib Toys

The best toys for use in the crib are those that can't roll or fall beyond the baby's reach. Arrays that span the crib from side to side provide a veritable workshop of activities for the child with knobs that twist, bulbs that squeeze, and gizmos that swing. These fascinating devices – virtually a new art form – entice children to investigate and explore, and in so doing, promote visual acuity and hand-eye coordination. A good grasping array will provide objects that give slightly under the child's grasp and return to their original position when released.

You might even make your own simple crib toys. Little skill is needed to attach a toy to a string stretched across the crib then, with another string, attach either the toy or the string to the baby's sleeve. The child will soon learn delightedly that by moving a particular limb he can make the toy move. (Perhaps the arm to which the string is attached would favor right-handedness or left-handedness, though I know of no studies on the matter.) The child will eventually enjoy toys he can drop over the side of his crib and haul back up by an attached string. If the objects rattle or make some sort of noise when they are dropped, all the better.

The Playpen

When children begin crawling, at about eight months of age, many new learning opportunities become available if youngsters aren't confined to a playpen. There are probably times when the use of a playpen makes sense, but playpens all too easily become infant jails. If you have a pet you wish to keep away from the baby, you could work out a time-share program for them: the animal spends half the time in the playpen, your heir spends the other half.

A baby's safety is of paramount importance. But instead of confining a youngster to a playpen, install protective devices around the home that shield him from danger while giving him freedom to explore. Install a folding gate across any open stairwell and a self-closing mechanism on any door leading to a staircase. Insert plastic caps into electrical outlets. Cordon off, in some way, electrical outlets into which appliances must remain plugged. Plastic locking devices are available that allow cupboard doors to open only far enough for adults to press the release. On the other hand, a child should be allowed to open cupboards that don't contain dangerous or breakable items.

Look around your home and ask yourself what objects the child could tip over, capsize, break, or cause to fall on top of him. If you live higher than ground level, childproof the balcony. Could the child squeeze between the balcony railings? Remember, most explanations of home accidents involving children begin with the words, "Who'd have thought he could ..." It is a parent's duty to consider even the most improbable and bizarre cause of accident.

Infants must not be scolded for being inquisitive or explorative. To do so would stifle those attributes that promote intellectual growth. If the crawling infant encounters something he could damage, or something that could harm him, the parent hasn't properly childproofed the home. Granted, childproofing is an inconvenience, but a child must be free to move if he is to be considered anything more than a favored prisoner around the home.

Perhaps a word would be in order on the matter of crawling. Some authorities believe that learning to crawl plays an important role in the development of intelligence. Babies are seen to move across the floor in different ways. The all-fours crawl – with opposite hands and knees moving forward at almost the same time – is thought to stimulate intellectual growth (in contrast with shifting forward with the legs while in a sitting position). Crawling provides a welcome opportunity for your child to vacate his seat or crib, so place your baby on a blanket on the floor occasionally and encourage him to crawl.

When children eventually learn to climb and begin walking by clinging to furniture, a new range of potential dangers must be foreseen and guarded against. And when, at last, he is able to toddle without holding the furniture for support, your highly mobile child has an even greater opportunity to harm himself.

The word *No!* has its uses. Though *No!* doesn't offer a reason for halting any action (an explanation the child probably wouldn't understand anyway), *No!* can stop an infant from touching objects that are difficult to shield him from without building fences around the home: items such as lamps, heaters, the stove and its dials. When your child is able to understand simple explanations, he should be taught that certain items can harm him or can be easily broken by him. At that time, *No!* should be accompanied by an explanation. By giving your child reasons for your restrictions, you encourage reasoning, and this, of course, promotes intelligence. But until that great moment arrives, *No!* will discourage a youngster from eating soap, toothpaste and other inedible items and from throwing toys or other objects or floating them in the toilet bowl.

Apropos the toilet bowl: children – not nature – decide when it is time to stop wetting their pants. Toilet training has never been the same since *Toilet Training in Less Than a Day* by Nathan H. Azrin and Richard M. Foxx was published in the mid 1970s. Few children could resist the author's Madison Avenue highly-motivated approach, and countless parents were able to escape a messy procedure and face life anew. Several books are now available and are easily found by typing the above book title into a search engine.

Here, then, are the important first considerations for your child from baby to toddler.

1 - Keep your child close, preferably in body contact.

2 - Construct mobiles and position them for easy viewing.

3 - Talk, talk, talk to your baby.

4 - Build your child's listening vocabulary and keep a list of the words taught.

5 - Provide bedding for the infant within sight of you, not in a quiet, dark room. Soothing music with a heartbeat tempo will promote contented sleep.

6 – Childproof your home.

4

A Word from the Experts

The purpose of this book is to show you how to raise your child's intelligence to the level of genius. Not surprisingly, your child will be different from other children – in a word, *smarter*. But there are some who think this is not a proper goal, and not a natural one: an opinion often held by authorities in education who seemingly believe that 'average' is God's will for children, and not something to be messed with.

The parents of Bentham, Mill, Witte, Kelvin, Berle, Wiener – and in our own time, Stern – all 'messed' with that supposed divine plan. Moreover, each voiced the outrageous conviction that they could achieve the same goal with any child – *yours!* Ultimately, you are the one who must decide what is right for your child, but in pursuing the goals of the program presented here, you are not likely to have the experts cheering for you.

Current standards in education tend to perpetuate the levels of intelligence and achievement we see on all sides, and because educational authorities lack the advanced information you now possess – namely, that children are capable of infinitely greater academic achievement when they are suitably taught – we are unlikely to see any improvements in public schooling.

Because the 'experts' often hold dazzling titles and impressive credentials, it seems wise to discuss the fallacies they sometimes voice, if only to assure you that you are pursuing a worthy and commendable goal.

Having gained considerable experience in other fields before I entered education, my view of its workings differs from that of most educators. In assessing the amount of time, effort, and excellence of performance demanded in other fields to win respect and authority, I find no equivalent effort or knowledge is needed in education to secure the title of expert. I realize this statement might earn me a charge of self-aggrandizement, but it's a risk I must run.

I have found that those holding prominent positions in education and child guidance – usually educational psychologists and developmental psychologists – seem content with the low levels of achievement we see among children. We are told that children are not capable of performing this or that activity or of understanding some other matter.

To illustrate, one prominent researcher in the field of epistemology – the science that deals with how knowledge is acquired – has concluded that a five-month-old infant won't be able to retrieve a hidden object unless some part of it is left showing. Another authority on early childhood behavior states that babies won't be able to roll over unaided much before five or five-and-a-half months. Yet, one youngster known to me could locate a totally hidden object at age one month and was able to roll over unaided at age three months. How could the child possibly accomplish this? *His mother taught him how.*

In a test to establish children's understanding, a well-known psychologist shows a child a tall, narrow container and a short, wide one. Both containers are capable of holding the same volume of liquid. This is demonstrated to the child by pouring the liquid back and forth between the vessels. Yet, when a very young child is asked which vessel holds more, he invariably picks the taller vessel. He will, researchers declare, until he reaches the age of about eight.

What the researchers fail to realize is that they are merely engaging the youngster in a vocabulary test or, if you prefer, a game of words: a game in which the child can only lose because his understanding of words is primitive and imprecise. "Which holds more?" The trick word here is 'more'. To an adult, the word 'more' has a precise meaning which children cannot know until they are taught.

In a child's limited experience, *height* is frequently a condition of *more*. To illustrate, a single-scoop cone topped with two scoops of ice cream contains more ice cream than a cone with a single scoop. *And the ice cream is higher!* And when a child builds a tower of blocks, more blocks go into a higher tower than a lower tower. Indeed, of the various mounds that children encounter, be they mounds of stones, toys, or food, the higher the mound, the more items are in it.

Children are quick to learn the meaning of *more*, requesting, as they often do, more of this or that food, or imploring the parent to persist in some playful activity with them. But children don't encounter the words *taller* and *higher* nor learn their respective meanings until later. Until that time when children learn where *taller* and *higher* take over attributes they thought were covered by the umbrella term *more*, children will continue to think that anything that is *higher* is also *more*.

In short, for a young child, *more* has a quality of height built into it. But teach a child the meaning of *taller* or *higher* and the child will gain, as a bonus, a more precise understanding of the word *more*.

If vocabulary enrichment takes place early, as was done with John Stuart Mill, Lord Kelvin, Norbert Wiener and the other bright youngsters mentioned earlier, children will know that the word *more* is unsuitable for describing the relative contents of the two containers, and they will do this long before the age of eight. Children's understanding of every scientific concept hinges on their understanding of words. Unfortunately, researchers fail to mention that their findings and conclusions are valid only for parents who sit back and contribute no more to their youngster's early education than the researchers and parents contributed to the children they studied.

Consider another. A much quoted researcher has concluded, from his extensive study of early intellectual ability and its ultimate influence on adult performance, that in terms of an individual's measurable life-long intelligence, 50 percent of the intellectual development has already taken place by age four, and 80 percent by age eight. The trouble with these figures is that they lead us to believe we have been presented with a natural law when in fact they merely describe an environmental consequence.

True, a child's ethical values, character traits, and personality are largely formed – if not immutably so – during the child's first few years. But this doesn't mean a child's intellectual limit has also been fixed. Studies show that our brain possesses a continuing potential for development. This attribute, called *plasticity* (discussed in Chapter 17), permits our brain to begin growth anew if circumstances favor or encourage it.

Deceptively, the figures of 50 percent and 80 percent do not indicate the extent to which intelligence has been *fixed*, but rather the extent to which it has been *arrested* by the child's environment. It is the child's *environment* that becomes stabilized early, *not* the child's potential for intellectual growth. What is stabilized is the *improbability of any improvement occurring in the quality and quantity of information to which the youngster is routinely exposed.* A home in which conversation dwells on sport and neighborhood-municipal-national gossip isn't likely to blossom forth with scientific inquiry. The television programs *Nova* or *National Geographic* and other scientific presentations are not likely to replace the cartoon-comedies. But – and here's the magical twist – engage a child in intellectually stimulating activities, introduce him to a brighter circle of peers, challenge his thinking, and you will see a more intelligent child emerge. That same elevating recipe holds for adults too, doesn't it?

The experts in all cases mentioned above are well known, hold, or held, prestigious positions with universities and have authored books to guide parents. But that was just a warm-up. For the strangest misdirection in education, we must turn to the field of reading instruction. Most educators (and the general public) are stumped by the mysteries presented in teaching children to understand print. This opens the door for almost anyone to step forward, speak convincingly, and hold teachers in awe while spouting absolute nonsense. Far fetched? Listen to a couple of experts.

One man – the most influential voice in North American education during the 1970s and 80s, author of nine books on education – held the population in thrall with his laid-back approach to learning. He avoided the difficulties of teaching reading by asserting that children didn't need to be taught to read. They would teach themselves to read, he claimed, if they really felt the desire. This amazing notion prompted many parents to sit and wait for the event to happen. It didn't.

And another, a specialist in reading instruction writes, "Guessing [while reading] has a bad reputation in education and especially among reading teachers…Guessing…is the most efficient manner in which to read and learn to read," and "..a good reader is quite likely to make quite conspicuous misreadings sometimes, like reading 'apartment' rather than 'house.'…This is the way fluent readers read." These are the words of a former Professor of Language in Education, an influential voice in reading technology who writes books and travels the continent lecturing schoolteachers. Picture, if you will, a former pupil of this approach to reading, now a practicing surgeon who operates 'by the book', engaged in an abdominal procedure, and misreading "remove the vesicles" as "remove the testicles." The doctor might have an eye-popping surprise for his revived patient.

Teachers and parents alike are lulled into a mesmeric state of acceptance by newspaper reports from educational dilettantes heavily mantled with impressive titles. A professor at the University of Florida states that more than half of the children entering Grade 1 are not ready to begin reading, and some shouldn't start until they are age nine. What might the parents of Witte, Bentham, Sidis, and the others think of this notion? To show that the U.S. has no monopoly on flawed thinking, a costly and extensive report prepared for the minister of education in Ontario stated the three Rs are no longer prerequisites for living together in society. The principal researcher asserted, "One of the essentials in our schools is how a student can develop a value system that ennobles him." I used to collect these quaint newspaper reports until I concluded, dispiritedly, that the field of education offered great promise for almost any ill-informed dabbler to spout rubbish, and the general public, knowing even less than he did, would usually swallow it whole.

But now, a final instance, perhaps the saddest and the most telling of all.

I appeared on a TV talk show with an internationally famous psychologist, chairman in a department of child study at a major university, author of several books dealing with children and child development. This man, let's call him Dr. Dave, warns parents in his books of the dangers inherent in advancing their children's early knowledge and skills – just the opposite of what I advise. During the interview, Dr. Dave asserted that preschool reading was of no value, that the skill was soon forgotten, and that children gained nothing by the process. I corrected him by stating the opposite was true, citing two long investigations by a well-known researcher, reported in the book *Children Who Read Early,* by Dolores Durkin. The author concluded, and her studies confirmed, that children who could read before they started school led their classes all through school (p. 133 in the hardbound edition).

Dave's reply? "She's recanted those findings."

The next day I wrote the author of *Children Who Read Early* to ask if she had changed her opinion. Certainly *not*, she replied.

Can we believe that Dave, a highly regarded authority – virtually an educational godfather to possibly millions of puzzled parents – had knowingly lied? Let's just say he protected his turf. With an established reputation, the respect of his professional associates and colleagues at stake, a lucrative private practice, and an enviable sale of books describing the children he had examined, my voiced correction must have struck him like a bullet in the head – or at least in the wallet. Obviously, the man hadn't studied the matter on which he was posing as an expert, so he fabricated. Naturally, his claim made me appear ill informed, but, as everyone knows, education sometimes carries a heavy price. I paid it. (But I'll know better next time.)

In homes where learning is valued, where many books are found, and where intellectual matters are discussed, such homes provide a natural intelligence-raising program. Consider the old-world equivalent of such a home, where, wealth aside, the heir's most valuable legacy wasn't quality of blood but lucidity of thought and caliber of speech. When Thomas Macaulay was four years old, a maidservant accidentally spilled hot coffee on his legs. Asked about his condition a little later, the youngster replied, "Thank you, Madam, the agony is abated." Such a response today might provoke thigh-slapping laughs, but it reveals the uncommonly high level of conversation to which the child had been exposed. As we will learn later, an early rich vocabulary and high intelligence are inseparable. It is not surprising that Macaulay became an eminent scholar and statesman. Similarly, considering the stimulating conversations to which Bertrand Russell, Winston Churchill and Franklin Roosevelt were privy – and conversations they engaged in with knowledgeable family members and brilliant visitors to their homes – it is hardly surprising that each achieved high intelligence without resort to a program such as the one presented in this book. The goal here is to give all children an advantage that in the past was available to only a privileged few.

But now, let's turn to those who really get things done in education: the schoolteachers. Schoolteachers are the industrious, dedicated force that keeps our educative systems working. Forget the glitzy electronic hardware and expensive teaching aids; it is the labor of teachers alone that provides a solid base for learning. But it's tough work. If teachers didn't feel so strongly about children, many might opt for 9:00 to 5:00 office jobs. Meetings I had with educational directors for three of Toronto's school boards a few years ago increased my respect for teachers. But we need to backtrack first.

Everyone agrees that whatever criticism might be voiced of public schooling, the incidence of faulty reading ability attracts the hottest fire. If children can't read well, every avenue of learning is closed to them or at least made difficult. And when children don't read well, teachers get the blame. But teachers are seldom able to choose the reading programs they use. Educational administrators pick them. But – and it's a tragic truth – administrators have rarely taught a child to read and have no first-hand knowledge of the problems faced in teaching this skill.

Consider, if educational administrators had access to a reading program so simple that even two-year-olds could be taught to read, you might expect them to grasp it joyfully and make it available to their teachers. Media people might be climbing over each other to get first-grabs on an earth-shaking story: **SCHOOL BOARD ENDS ILLITERACY**. But when I offered to adapt the no-fail Institute reading program to the needs of the public school classroom, I encountered only apathy. In fact, one director excused himself and left me talking to a subordinate.

Fruitless meetings with educational directors in three cities left me marveling at the achievements of schoolteachers when they are backed by unconcerned and unenterprising leaders.

The sad extent of bureaucratic contrariness and ineptitude in educational management is told by former U.S. Secretary of Education William J. Bennett in his book *The De-Valuing of America*: a chilling report on the whole iceberg of educational malpractice, of which my few encounters were merely tips.

After decades of dealing with movers and shakers in education, I have concluded that little learning or drive is needed to plant a secure foot on the administrative ladder. Tragic though it is, the chances for improvement are not great. B.F. Skinner (whose work *The Technology of Teaching* is sadly neglected) expressed only faint hope when he stated candidly, "Education is not likely to improve because no heads will roll if it doesn't improve."

5

Your Child's Speech

A child's ability to speak and express his thoughts comes as a great relief to parents. At last, the child can tell what ails him, can tell whether his stomach or head hurts, can tell if he has been well treated by others in the parents' absence, and can report on other important matters. But babbling comes first.

Babbling is a form of pre-speech often well lubricated with saliva (deaf infants, however, don't babble; they merely make strange sounds). Encourage your infant to babble. Show your appreciation and delight. "Hey, Lana, I think Wendall's reciting poetry. It's iambic meter. OK, Wendall, let Mommy hear it."

Psychologists who deal with early childhood can predict, within rough limits, the age at which your child will be able to sit, crawl, walk with assistance, and finally walk unaided. And there isn't much that parents can do to hasten these developments. First, bone, muscle, and connective tissue must grow, and parents have little control over such growth. However, when developmental psychologists predict the age at which a child will begin talking – as some do – their predictions are based on the performance of children whose parents little-guessed their children's potential or what he or she could achieve if they, the parents, stopped listening to experts.

One celebrated authority on children's first three years of life reports that children will begin speaking their first *words* between twelve and fourteen months. But Aaron Stern's daughter Edith was speaking in simple *sentence* form at eleven months. Magic? Genius? No, her father coached her in learning to speak.

It will be obvious now that you alone establish whether your child will begin to speak early or later. When he speaks and how well he speaks will depend on how much time you spend talking to him, building his listening vocabulary, and encouraging him to mouth pre-speech sounds (the nonsense sound-combinations that children create before they speak proper words).

Your child will understand many words before he gains sufficient control of his speech muscles to get his own lips and tongue around those words. To make talking easier for your child, encourage him to voice single-syllable words first: *toe, soap, tub, hat,* and so on; then gradually introduce some two-syllable words: *baby, water.*

Children's first attempts at speech are, of course, amusing. 'Water' becomes *wawa*; 'juice' becomes *oos*, and so on. There is always a temptation to use the child's own simplified version of English when speaking to him. Resist the temptation. To ask a child if he would like some *wawa* would present a distorted model for him to copy. When your child says *wawa*, treat his effort as a great accomplishment, while reinforcing the correct pronunciation of the word.

"Yes, good. Zinnia said *water*. Good girl, Zinnia. Well, let's get some *water* then. Here we are, w*ater*."

"Oos."

"Oh, it's *juice* you want. My mistake. Good girl. Zinnia can say *juice*. Here we are, then. Drink your *juice*."

"Wawa."

The parents of Karl Witte and Edith Stern scrupulously avoided baby talk when teaching their children to speak: a practice that has been honored in the early education of all those who eventually became eminent. Terms such as *bow-wow, doggie, pussycat, tum-tum,* and *jammies* can only hinder correct speech development.

Though we need be wary of television and radio as teaching aids, each can play a part in advancing your child's speech. Television provides a better form of instruction than radio because your child can see the speaker's lips move. An interview program suits the need admirably, and a weather channel provides both voice and movement. It goes without saying that violence should be avoided.

As your child's speech advances, he will begin to form two-word sentences: *Too hot, More please, All gone.* In time, three-word sentences will follow: *Haven't got it, Dolly not here,* and gradually progress to correct, simple sentences: *I like peanut butter, My daddy's a policeman, What's your name?*

Though your child may not be speaking words at three weeks as the Susedik children did, nor sentences at eleven months as Edith Stern was able to do, you might expect him or her to be speaking sentences by eighteen months. Some children will acquire this ability earlier, others later. Some youngsters experience difficulty learning to speak, and for reasons that aren't understood, they are usually boys. Albert Einstein, for example, was slow to talk. Einstein's speech was so backward at age four that his parents thought he might be mentally retarded. Even at age nine, young Albert still lacked skill in speaking. Unfortunately, we will never know to what extent Einstein's speech difficulties might have been avoided by the procedures described here.

Encouraging a child to speak must always be a cheerful procedure. What profit would there be if a youngster, in learning to speak, lost a carefree, smiling parent? A baby's first need is warm, loving support.

If you have been blessed with twins then the instruction given here doubles in importance. And that's not just a gag. Twins have a social advantage over other children because there is always someone for them to play with. On the other hand, they face an intellectual disadvantage by being constantly in the company of someone who knows no more than they do. Though twins are able to entertain themselves, they learn nothing from each other's babble. They therefore have greater need for the company of an attentive adult. Studies show that infants who associate mainly with other infants will not develop verbal skills as early as infants who are constantly in the company of adults.

Matters are usually much improved for a single first-born child. A first-born child wins uncontested parental attention. He or she becomes the king or queen of the household. Everything revolves around the baby. He is fussed over, tickled and petted. And, most importantly, he is constantly in the presence of those who know more than he does and can teach him. That is why first-born children are often brighter than second- or third-born children who must compete with their predecessors for parental attention. Also, parents burdened with greater expenses because of their enlarged family may have less time to give later arrivals.

Bilingualism

Many believe that learning two languages is intellectually stimulating; however, studies do not support this conclusion. Bilingual children often obtain lower scores on verbal intelligence tests than do monolingual children. Learning two languages at the onset of speech has been found to produce confusion in the use of languages. In homes where two languages are frequently mixed – meaning, where parents employ words from both languages in their conversations – a young child encounters difficulty in differentiating the two languages and may be overwhelmed by the confusing similarities and inconsistencies of what appears to be a single language. A second language is best learned after the primary language is firmly established.

Convenience Education

As we have seen, some parents of the past have gone to great lengths to advance their children's knowledge and elevate their intelligence. But most parents today haven't the time to engage in a similarly extensive teaching program with their youngsters. Some mothers must place their child in the care of others on weekdays. Other parents can stay home for two, three, or more years with their child or children. To serve the greatest number of parents, we will put a hypothetical limit on the length of time a mother stays home with her youngster. We'll assume that you, having stayed home with your child for a year and a half, must now return to your job. We will further assume that your child will be spending the weekdays with friends or neighbors, or at a daycare center. Choosing a suitable daycare center for your child is an important decision. After all, the daycare environment can supplement your home-education program, or undermine it. (Selecting a suitable daycare center is covered in Chapter 14).

Whichever you choose – friends, neighbors, or daycare – leaving your child in the care of others introduces him or her to random ambient instruction (discussed in Chapter 1). Without meaning to, every child and adult your child now encounters and spends time with will become his or her teacher. This doesn't spell disaster to your educational program; it does, however, introduce competition. And with competition, your instruction, after hours and on weekends, becomes more important.

Our purpose now is to give your child an enriched education in the limited time you have for instruction. To this end, we will turn the moments you engage in housework, and while eating, while traveling, and while shopping to your child's educational gain.

Let's begin with mealtimes.

Couples usually establish a mealtime routine long before their first child arrives. Perhaps they watch TV. Perhaps they discuss their health, the state of the bank account, the car, the neighborhood, and other matters. The arrival of a third voice at the table – the child's – prompts, in many homes, little change in mealtime conversation. The parents either talk around the youngster or try to ignore him, and the child, thrilled at having finally acquired the ability to speak, is obliged to initiate conversation in whatever way he can. By introducing a program of education at mealtimes, parents can provide entertainment for themselves and for the child. When a parent shares mealtimes alone with a child, the need for such initiative becomes even greater.

Perhaps you like to read while eating. If so, fine, but read aloud, slowly and clearly, expanding on the text at every opportunity for your child's benefit. Or you might describe things. Describe how ketchup is made (or at least how you *think* it's made). Take your purse to the table and check its contents, explaining why you carry each item, where you got it, how much you paid, and so on. Give a brief rundown on the meal.

"This is porridge, Hector. It's made from oats. That's what horses eat."

The possibilities for conversation are limitless. Your child need not understand what you are talking about. It is the sound of your voice that pacifies and casts a reign of contentment on your attentive audience. Yet, mealtimes need not be given wholly to education. By inserting just occasional brief educating activities you can make the occasion more enjoyable for everyone. If you prefer not to talk while chewing, television can relieve you of the task. Cartoons are not a good choice because of the violence. A talk show is acceptable. An orchestral presentation is excellent, and if you were to acquire a videotape or compact disk of a musical concert your child will learn, by repeated showings, the various instruments, their workings, and their sounds.

Keeping a child occupied while driving can sometimes be difficult. However, if *you* don't initiate some form of activity, your child is apt to initiate his own. And if his creations are noisy and distractive, you will be less able to cope with the problems of driving – which could be particularly upsetting when driving conditions are bad. Engaging a youngster in educating activities while driving can therefore help ensure a safe trip.

While driving, the constant change of scenery provides numerous subjects to comment on. "Look, Hector, there's a fire engine. Listen to the noise. That's a siren. Hold tight. Daddy says I'd be great in the Indianapolis 500. Oops, a policeman. Slow down."

Drivel? Of course! But we're not striving for a gold medal in elocution. Your youngster will delight in just hearing the sound of your voice.

If you travel by public transit, your monologue may have to be restrained. Hold up your child so he can look out the window. With someone else handling the task of driving, you can give full attention to the passing scene.

Shopping provides many new and different opportunities for comment. A supermarket offers great potential for chatter. With your infant on your back – papoose fashion – you would have both hands free to select items. Perhaps your youngster could grasp and carry something that wouldn't break or bruise if dropped.

As you see, education can proceed effectively and uninterruptedly while you attend to the routine tasks every parent faces; while you deal with household chores, while you eat, drive, and shop: moments that might otherwise be trying. There is still another little-guessed way of advancing your child's knowledge that – best of all – doesn't require your time and attention. Tutors.

Educational Babysitters

Hiring tutors isn't new. Wealthy families have traditionally hired tutors to teach their children if, indeed, they didn't own slaves as the Romans did to fill this role. Fortunately, neither wealth nor slaves are needed today to acquire tutors. Low-cost tutors are abundant and easily found when you know how. One single-parent hired no fewer than twenty-three tutors, aged nine to sixteen, to supervise his children during a six-year home-instruction period. As an added attraction, their services eventually included supervising the children's bath and tooth brushing.

When both parents are employed outside the home, the advantages of hiring tutors will be obvious. Even in homes where the mother is home all day with one or more youngster, a temporary release from the children can be welcome. Moreover, children often show greater enthusiasm for learning when taught by an outsider. One mother attempted for years to teach her son to swim. When an older youngster took on the task, her son was swimming in a month.

How do you find suitable tutors? A popular babysitter makes a likely candidate. Girls who are in demand as babysitters have probably proved themselves to be reliable, responsible, relaxed and comfortable with children. Boys make good babysitters too, though if your child is female, you may prefer to entrust her care to a girl rather than a boy. Children who perform well in school are potentially good tutors. They may already have been called upon in school to help slower pupils, or they may have been 'borrowed' by teachers of lower grades to help as teaching monitors. Ask children in your neighborhood for the names of top students in their class, then speak to those named about your teaching needs. One suitable tutor will often lead you to another because the girl's best friend will likely have the same good qualities you are looking for.

What should these qualities be? The English philosopher John Locke described the ideal tutor in 1693.

> *Seek out somebody that may know how discreetly to frame his manners: place him in hands where you may, as much as possible, secure his innocence, cherish and nurse up the good, and gently correct and weed out any bad inclinations, and settle in him good habits. This is the main*

point, and this being provided for, learning may be had in the bargain.*

You would need only show the tutor what material your child has been working with and let her take over. If your child is still learning to speak single-syllable words, the tutor could engage in a playful exercise that entices repetition and improvement. Make a list of the words you want the tutor to work with. If two-syllable words are the order, provide a list of the ones your child has mastered plus a few others for the tutor to teach. Tutors will have a more important role to fill later when your child advances.

How much should you pay tutors? The law of supply and demand will influence the cost, but generally, the rate will depend on the tutor's age (and how desperate you are to secure relief from the unceasing demands of parenting at the end of a tough day). If a tutor is old enough to baby-sit, then he or she is accustomed to receiving a stipulated amount per hour for sitting and watching television, or for completing homework, or for just lounging around. So, for teaching, your tutor might be paid more than a babysitting rate. Children who are too young to baby-sit (perhaps younger than age twelve) will welcome the opportunity to earn money, and they can be hired for the prevailing babysitting rate or possibly less. By finding suitable nine-, ten-, and eleven-year-olds (some of whom have a genius for charming small children), you can secure excellent tuition for your youngster at low cost.

More important than a tutor's age is his or her maturity. What degree of maturity will be needed to guide your child? That depends on your youngster's age and temperament. Usually, preschool-age children are easily managed by a nine- or ten-year-old; however, if there are two preschoolers, you may need an older tutor. If your child is six, seven, or eight years old, he or she will be more effectively taught by children who more nearly fill the image of an adult; say, age fifteen or sixteen.

How many tutors will you need? That will depend on how many times a week you want your child to be taught by others. Much of the pleasure of teaching can be lost if a tutor teaches more than twice a week. Better, therefore, to secure several tutors. Pick times for your child's instruction that suit both you and the tutors: after school, or after supper, and perhaps on Saturday and Sunday mornings. Instruction shouldn't be scheduled for a time your child would normally engage in some other favored activity because this could arouse resentment for your teaching program.

* *Some Thoughts Concerning Education*, John Locke (New York, 1964)

If your tutors are responsible enough to also fill the role of true babysitter, you will be able to run errands, shop, or visit a neighbor while your child or children are being taught. If your child is already old enough to attend school and you and your spouse work outside the home, the tutor, given a key, could teach your child after school until someone arrives home.

These various activities, teaching while attending to housework, while eating, while shopping, while traveling, and by the service of young tutors, constitutes convenience education; educating, yes, but in a manner that makes life easier for you while advancing your child's intelligence.

Now, let's consider what subjects your child should be taught. John Locke said, "When he can talk, 'tis time he should learn to read." Locke believed, however, that children should be taught to read in a fun-filled way. That is the approach we will use.

6

Teaching Children to Read

The brain is an organ not a muscle; yet, strangely, the brain responds to usage and challenge as if it were a muscle. Dealing with complicated tasks triggers physical and chemical changes in brain cells, or neurons as they are called. Of the various ways the brain might be burdened, learning to read is among the most challenging. The task of interpreting small squiggles on paper – sound symbols – is similar to solving an immense, intricate puzzle; one that, piece by piece, must be learned and fitted correctly into place to create a mental picture of what the writer had in mind. Having solved this complex puzzle at a remarkably young age might explain why John Markwell, mentioned in Chapter 1, acquired the outstanding intellectual power that gave him permanent academic supremacy.

Learning to read is the equivalent of a brain massage, which is why reading instruction begins at the Institute as soon as children enter the program. Very young children – two-year-olds – are sometimes not yet speaking when they are enrolled or they may be speaking a language other than English. These children learn to speak English at the same time they are learning to read it.

Much of the reading instruction given at the Institute is one-to-one, which means that each child receives about four or five minutes of individual instruction in the morning and again in the afternoon (if the child attends all-day). You, on the other hand, will be able to spend longer with your child. He or she can therefore be expected to advance more quickly.

Your child may be age two, three, four or even older. Before pursuing his or her rise to literacy, let's review the reasons for, and the benefits of, engaging a youngster in an early reading instruction program.

Reading instruction has traditionally taken place in North America about four years after children learn to speak. But this delay is neither necessary nor desirable. For centuries, perceptive parents have asserted and demonstrated that as soon as children can understand the meaning of voiced words, they can and should be taught to interpret those words in printed form. There are several good reasons for – and some little-guessed advantages to be gained by – teaching youngsters to read long before the age of six.

The first and most obvious advantage is the enjoyment reading adds to childhood. Children who can read signs, labels, and posters when they are taken along on shopping excursions find greater pleasure than those who can't read. Being naturally inquisitive, children yearn to know what is going on around them and, surrounded as we are by print in an urban environment, the ability to read is the equivalent of, and as valuable as, a sixth sense.

Teaching children to read permits them to enlarge their vocabularies more easily and, as we have seen, intelligence is closely related to size of vocabulary. Another important benefit: children who can read books aren't dependent on the presence and mood of an adult for the enjoyment of their favorite stories. Nor are they wholly dependent on television for their entertainment (which, by survey, averages 23.5 hours a week for children younger than five). And the reading of bedtime stories becomes more pleasurable for youngsters when they can take turns reading with parents.

Another often overlooked advantage: the world becomes a safer place for children who can interpret the meanings of FIRE ESCAPE, DANGER, BEWARE OF DOG, POISON, KEEP OUT, and other warnings.

The two studies conducted by Dolores Durkin, reported in Chapter 4, revealed the intimate link that exists between early reading ability and eventual academic success. Not surprisingly, early readers usually excel in whatever field they eventually choose. A study of 400 eminent men and women described in *Cradles of Eminence* led the researchers (Goertzel & Goertzel) to report that, as children, the 400 showed their greatest superiority in reading ability; that many of them were already reading by age four.

In a study of twelve children having IQs of 180 or higher, Dr. Leta Hollingworth found the group had been taught to read at an average age of three, the latest, at four years. And Lewis Terman and Melita Oden noted, in comparing eighty-one children with IQs of 170 or higher, that their youngsters began reading between the ages of three and five.

Perhaps these children were reading early because they were bright – a tempting belief. However, a study of super-bright children (IQs 120-200) reported in the book *Able Misfits*, by M.L. Kellmer Pringle, found that one-third of the brilliant youngsters were reading *below* their actual or chronological age which, of course, was far below their intellectual ages. Bright children, and average children too – and yes, even slow children – learn to read early if, and only if, someone teaches them to read, or if parents or other children provide sufficient clues so youngsters can puzzle out the intricacies of reading on their own.

> ## The General's Burden
>
> Father of the famous general George Patton IV did not believe children should be taught to read until they were adolescents. Kept home and taught other matters by his parents and an aunt, George finally attended school at age twelve, an illiterate. The price of this long delay was steep. He never learned to read well.

The most compelling reason for teaching preschoolers to read – intellectual advancement aside for the moment – is that there isn't any valid reason for denying them so simple, yet so valuable, a skill, especially when there is no guarantee youngsters will be well taught when they eventually attend school. The child who can already read on entering Grade 1 is the only child in the class to whom literacy is guaranteed if the teacher is burdened with a slow, faulty reading program.

Consider, in comparison with learning to read, learning to speak is a far more difficult task for youngsters: one that takes a year or more. Learning to read, on the other hand, takes only two or three months when a simplified reading program is used. (In a case reported in *Teach Your Child to Read in Just Ten Minutes a Day*, one child was reading after only eleven days of instruction.)

Can we wonder that children age six and seven often show little interest in learning to read when the skill has been needlessly delayed for so long? After learning to speak at age two, four years must pass before they finally receive reading instruction. Not surprisingly, youngsters have by then developed a life-style that doesn't depend on literacy. They have learned to get along without interpreting sound squiggles on a page; so why bother? There is television, video games, and conversation to take the place of reading. To exacerbate the problem, reading instruction employs a language that children were using as infants: "Look, I see a dog."

And yet, despite the dangers inherent in delay, some individuals posing as experts warn against teaching preschoolers to read, saying,

"Let children be children. Let them enjoy childhood," as if by teaching children a simple skill their preschool pleasures will be arrested or diminished.

Strange ideas have gripped the educational community and if parents aren't prepped on the absurdities they can encounter, the parent's best intentions can be derailed by seemingly impressive bafflegab. Consider the following method used in some public schools to determine whether or not a child should receive reading instruction.

Reading Readiness

'Reading readiness' tests are used to tell teachers whether children are ready to read. Children who score low on 'readiness' tests are considered unready. Their instruction is deferred until a later date when they can perform better on the test.

How can a child fail a reading-readiness test? By inattention to detail. In one test, children are asked to detect small differences seen in illustrations. A drawing of a house, a gingerbread man, a rabbit, and a pig might be shown down one side of a sheet of paper, one beneath the other. Beside the house, running across the page, would be three more houses. But some detail would be missing from each of these houses. One of the houses might have a window and a chimney missing. Another might have the door missing and have no smoke issuing from the chimney. The third house might have two windows and a doorknob missing. In a similar way, the gingerbread man, the rabbit, and the pig would be accompanied by three similar figures with various parts missing. Children are then asked to detect and draw in with a pencil the missing parts. To whatever extent children fail to notice missing parts they are said to be unready for reading. Pseudo scientific testing of this sort misguides teachers and makes their job all the more difficult.

Panic in the Home

British writer Sir Compton Mackenzie disclosed that his mother, in desperation, took his younger brother to a specialist because he still wasn't reading by age four. She herself had been reading by age two-and-a-half and young Compton was reading at one year, ten months.

Children are sometimes thought to teach themselves to read. That's an important point, so let's look at it. Occasionally, newspapers report the case of a youngster who learned to read so easily that it challenges belief. One case sticks in my mind. Parents reported their child learned to read by studying the telephone book. They said they offered no help. There is no rational explanation for this astonishing event. The child apparently had a mystical genius for interpreting print – a genius comparable to that possessed by Chopin for creating music.

In most cases, however, when parents say their children taught themselves to read they mean they taught their youngster to read *without intending to*. That's an entirely different matter. What parents are saying is that they had neither plan nor desire to teach. They therefore had no reason to believe – or even to expect – that by reading to their child on their lap and running a finger along beneath the words, this could constitute instruction, nor that their child could learn from such faint clues. But, surprisingly, some children need little instruction – from parents or from playing school with an older reading child – to puzzle out the system for themselves without further guidance.

The Sound of Print

We read partly with our eyes and partly with our ears. Once this fact is recognized, teaching children to read becomes a simpler business. Limericks provide irrefutable proof that our ears play a major role in reading. Consider a limerick composed by Ogden Nash.

> One bliss for which
> There is no match
> Is when you itch
> To up and scratch.

We hear both the rhyme and the meter in our head when we read limericks, as you just did. That's why limericks are just as enjoyable when we read them as when we hear them spoken. You and I and all skillful readers assign sounds to letters on a page with great speed. These sounds play through our mind quickly as if on a tape recording.

The difference between skillful readers and poor readers is that skillful readers know the letter-sound code and can use it easily. We see the truth of this continually at the Institute with outside children who attend our reading clinic. When these youngsters arrive, they don't *read* words as you and I do, they *guess* them. Or they just stop, and give up. The word *elephant* stumps them because no one has told them that a *p* joined with an *h* can sometimes assume the sound of *f*.

The only time adults might ever notice they possess skill with the letter code is when they are obliged to give voice to names they have never seen or heard before, names such as Thredsborg, Crandelman, and Givsner. You are able to voice these sequences of printed letters because – and only because – you are practiced in interpreting letter-sounds. This same skill permits you to give voice to words you haven't heard before. Here are two for the record. Take them slowly: disproportionableness and the jawbreaker anti-interdenominational-istically.

Teaching children to read is simply a matter of giving them the same information you and I use daily. We need but teach youngsters the sounds that are normally assigned to letters, then encourage them to use this knowledge many times until they can decode words with the speed and precision you and I do. By such exercise, children gain the equivalent of a 'third ear', one that permits them to hear print. There is no magic involved. There is no mystery. And there is no failure. Never.

Critics of the letter-sound system of reading claim that English pronunciation is too irregular to establish firm rules for letter sounds, and they usually point to the various sounds that can be represented by the letters **ough**, as in *bough, bought, rough, cough, through*. But the consistency with which the **ough** combination is seized upon to prove their point is a testimony to the absence of any other letter combination having similarly erratic pronunciation.

Granted, there *are* irregularities in the English language, and assuredly, these variations could confuse a child if we thoughtlessly paraded them before the child's bewildered gaze. Who among us didn't mispronounce one or other of *viscount, yacht, island, magician*, or *epitome* the first time we encountered these words in print? But we muddled through, because approximately 85 percent of our language is entirely consistent with letter-sound rules we have all learned – learned, it should be noted, *not* by reciting rules, but by reading.

The rules that govern letter-sounds – singly or in combination – are sufficiently consistent that even misspelled words are identifiable when the substituted spellings are consistent with other letter-sound combinations. Prove this for yourself. What words are represented by *phyre, aiker, gnayl, lofe, kawmycks,* and *gnewed*?

Some rules of pronunciation are easier to learn than others. By introducing the easier letter-sound combinations to children first, and forgetting about the exceptions, we quickly give youngsters an understanding of the mechanics of reading. And when children see the magical effect produced by letters, and when they gain rudimentary skill in interpreting letter-sound values, we can gradually introduce the variations and exceptions.

The reading methods most commonly found in public schools are the letter-sound (phonic) method, the whole-word (look-say or look-

and-guess) method, and a mixture of the two, called 'language experience', which can be taught in a variety of ways depending on the teacher. Success of the language experience method varies, whereas the phonic method, when correctly taught, has no equal for speed and ease of learning. *All* children, even those who fail reading readiness tests – even *infants!* – soon become adventurous readers. (The term 'phony phonics' has been coined to describe incorrect letter-sound instruction.)

The next chapter presents a step-by-step program that may take two, three, or more months to complete. Most of the other chapters in the book contain material that is suitable for non-readers – including, strangely enough, Chapter 8, *Encouraging the Habit of Reading*. If you don't intend to teach your child to read immediately, or if he can already read, you might proceed with that other material.

7

How to Teach Your Child to Read

Teaching a child to read can take weeks, possibly months, depending on the amount of time you can give to instruction and practice. But reading is just one of several stimulating activities described in this book. Vocabulary enrichment (Chapter 9), solving mazes (page 129), the 'diligent spotter' activity (page 143), and memory enhancement (page 143): each will help speed your child to the goal of this program: rare intelligence. So, while you teach your child to read, learn about the other activities and include them in your program.

Huddle

I can understand the self-doubt that might grip anyone planning to – hoping to – teach a child to read. At one time, I too had never taught a child to read. But I bumbled on, just an ordinary parent with no experience, with no plan or textbook to guide me. To my surprise, I found the task astonishingly easy.

You have a tested program to use; one that includes a game to promote repetition in an entertaining way. You have built-in success. Take heart.

Look in the mirror and see a winner.

This chapter deals with instruction intended less for reading, more for following. You might skip the chapter until you actually begin teaching your child to read.

Repeated use of the terms 'your child' or 'your youngster' could become wearisome, so I will occasionally substitute children's names when describing the procedures.

Before starting to teach your child – let's call him Adlai – to read, study this entire chapter. Some matters mentioned later in the chapter will apply equally well to the beginning of your reading program.

Though the instruction is written for teaching children at home, schoolteachers might adapt the system for classroom use; however, full instructions for teaching in kindergarten and Grade 1 – including special games that capitalize on the presence of many children – are given in my book *Teach Your Child to Read in Just Ten Minutes a Day*. Instruction is also given there for supervisors of daycare centers and nursery schools and for babysitters.

In some homes, the parents alone will teach reading. In other homes, tutors will help. And in some homes, tutors may run the whole program. In the instruction that follows, the parent is seen as the sole teacher. If you intend to enlist tutors, interpret the text accordingly, guiding tutors and providing them with the lettered material. If your tutors are sufficiently mature, you might simply hand them this book, give them the necessary materials and let them handle the lettering themselves.

A Two-thousand-year-old Error

Though children are commonly taught the alphabet – and, indeed, even taught a song to make remembering it easier – knowing the names of the letters (*ay, bee, see, dee*) only serves to confuse children when they begin learning to read. This teaching error, which dates back to Greek and Roman days, has caused the unjust punishment of an incalculable number of children. Through the ages, schoolchildren were exhaustively drilled for a year or so in reciting the alphabet (indeed, both forwards and backwards!). Then, when they still proved unable to read, they were flogged for being obstinate by teachers who were themselves ignorant of the fact that there is little connection between the *names* of the letters and the ability to read. Today, children's television programs and schoolteachers alike naively perpetuate this teaching blunder.

Communicating with a Child

An important first consideration when teaching a child any subject is to use words the child knows and understands – which seems both simple and obvious doesn't it? Yet this error is easily overlooked because children aren't in the habit of stopping the speaker to ask what a word means. To illustrate, the question, "Can you think of another word that begins with the sound of *kuh*?" is meaningless to a child who doesn't understand the meaning of *another, word, begins,* or *sound.* The question might as well be asked in a foreign language. Be extremely careful, therefore, to avoid using words that could confuse your pupil. Study the list of words in Figure 9 on page 74 for words Adlai may not understand and teach him their meaning.

Learning the sounds of the letters (the letter-sound code) and knowing how to use these sounds is easier for children if they first learn to distinguish the sounds they hear in speech. Adults usually aren't aware that almost all spoken words are made up of more than one sound. For example, the word *cat* is a combination of three sounds: the throat-clearing sound of the *c* (*kuh* without voice given to the *uh* part), the voiced sound of *a*, and finally, the tongue-palate sound of *t* (simply a burst of palatal air with no voiced accompaniment).

We begin by teaching children the capital letters instead of lower case or 'small' letters. Why? Because when Adlai eventually begins to read, the first readable words he encounters – on cars, signs, and labels – will usually be printed in capital letters, and we would like to tempt him to use his newly acquired reading skill. A second reason: we don't want him assessing the shape of words to help identify them (called configuration clues in the look-say reading method). We want him to rely solely on the sounds of letter.

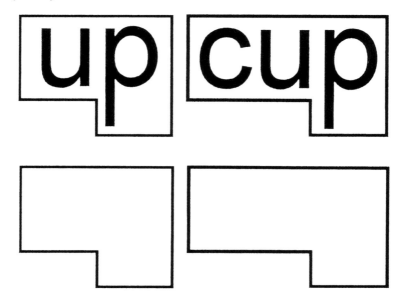

Figure 1: – *Configuration clues.*

Speech Sounds and Letter Sounds

Traditionally, the first letter children have been taught is the letter **A**. However, there is no inherent 'firstness' to **A** in the way we speak. Making the letter **C** our first letter will serve us better. Show Adlai the letter **C** on page 61 and tell him this shape tells us to make the throat-clearing sound (though not necessarily using the words *shape* or *sound* in your instruction) of *kuh*, but *without any voice or grunt* being given to the *uh* part.

Let's take this slowly because people sometimes have difficulty making the sound correctly without a recorded example to follow. Say the word 'tic'. Now say it again, this time, leave a space between the *ti* and the *c*. You will notice you don't use your voice for the *c*. That is the sound we want. Just a clearing of the back of the throat. Air alone makes this sound, not your voice. We will call this sound, and a few other sounds to be introduced, an *air sound* as apposed to a voiced sound.

Now, back to Adlai.

Have him run his finger around the **C** on page 61. "This tells us to say *kuh*." Encourage him to produce the unvoiced sound while tracing his finger around the letter a few times. Never refer to the letter by its name – which sounds like 'see'. Refer to it only by the *kuh* sound. If Adlai is already familiar with this shape – perhaps from watching television – and has already learned to call it by name ('see'), explain that the *name* of this shape and its *sound* are two different things. (And you may now be obliged to teach him the meaning of *name*, *sound*, and *different*.) Explain that though one animal is named a cat, it doesn't say 'cat,' it says meow. In the same way, though some shapes have the names 'ay,' 'bee,' 'see,' 'dee,' and so on, the shapes actually tell us to make different sounds.

Generally, children will more easily distinguish sounds heard at the beginning of words, so quiz Adlai on words that start with the *cuh* sound. "What sound does *car* begin with, Adlai?" He may not be able to distinguish the sound; so make it for him, pointing out that the large **C** tells us to make that sound. Have him repeat the sound. "What sound does *cow* start with?" Again, he may not know, so make the sound for him and have him repeat it. "Nice going, you're doing fine. What sound does *cat* begin with?" Again, he probably won't know, so tell him, and perhaps go back to *car*. But now, slowly *stutter* the beginning sound to help him. "What sound does *c-c-c-car* start with?" He may be able to identify the sound, but don't count on it. Have him produce the stuttered version of the word. Then proceed similarly, stuttering the beginning sound of *cow, cat, crib, cuddle, caterpillar, candy,* and the names of any

60

C A T

P N E

U I O

Figure 2: — *The letters here and on the following two pages are used to help children learn letters in preparation for reading.*

S B H

M G

L R D

FKW

VJX

YZQ

relatives, friends, or neighbors whose names begin with the *cuh* sound.

This business seems very simple to you and me, but we have dealt with millions – possibly billions – of printed words. Don't expect Adlai to develop skill until he has encountered a few thousand words.

Make a duplicate of the letter **C** using a wide felt-tip pen or brush and clip it onto the sun visor of your car. At mealtimes, prop up, or fix to the wall, the large **C**, and draw the child's attention to items that begin with the *cuh* sound. What sound does *c-c-c-cup* begin with, Adlai? And what about *c-c-c-can*?" Bring items to the table to use in your exercise of sound isolation: a camera, a candle, a can-opener. Or simply introduce appropriate words: *c-c-cowboy, c-c-carpet, c-c-curtain*, and so forth.

Identification of **C** might even become a mealtime game. Ask your youngster – Emerald – to try to find **C**s on packages and food labels (a game that can also be played when you are shopping at the supermarket), or bring a newspaper to the table and let her find **C**s in the headlines.

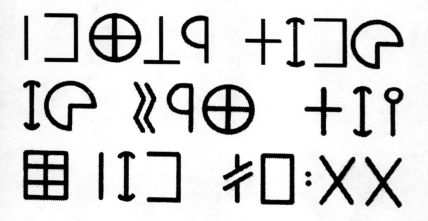

Figure 3: *Can you read this? Imagine how hard reading is for a child.*

You may be surprised at the difficulty she can experience in detecting the beginning sound of words. To understand the difficulty better, imagine being thrust into a society that uses sound symbols different from our own. Told that the plus sign (**+**) represents the sound of *cuh*, we wouldn't have much difficulty spotting two such symbols in a supposed sign at the supermarket (Fig. 3). This is a simple task for us because we have encountered and compared billions of printed symbols.

(You will make about 500,000 such comparisons just while reading this book.) A child who can detect the symbol **C** and assign the correct sound to it after seeing **C** only one or two hundred times deserves great praise. (In the interest of anagrammatical enquiry the sign says: FRESH CORN ON THE COB 6 FOR $100.)

Encourage Emerald, and be patient. Never show concern or disappointment (even though you might sometimes feel it) when she fumbles words. Instead, express delight and be quick to compliment her when she succeeds in isolating a sound. If you sometimes seem to 'jump out of your skin' with surprise and delight, she'll think the exercise is a lot of fun. "Emerald, you're doing just marvelously. Wait 'til Daddy sees what you can do." Emerald should develop three distinct and separate skills before you introduce a second letter.

1. She should be able to make the correct sound for **C** easily when she sees it.
2. She should be able to detect the *cuh* sound in spoken words beginning with that sound.
3. She should be able to pick out **C**s in printed text.

Emerald may take a week or two to accomplish these tasks, depending on how often you encourage her to try.

When she can easily locate **C**s in print, can sound them correctly, and can identify spoken words that begin with the *cuh* sound, show her the letter **A** on page 61. Have her trace around its shape several times with her finger while making the **A** sound (as heard in *rat*, not *rate*).

Make a duplicate of the letter **A**, clip it to the sun visor in the car and, while driving, quiz her from a list of simple words she knows – or can easily be taught – that begin with the *a* sound: perhaps *accident, ambulance, alligator, ant, apple, apartment, animal, astronaut*. These same words will serve for your mealtime quizzes too. "What sound does *a-a-a-apple* begin with, Emerald?"

Engage her in the same activities for **A** that you engaged her in for **C**. Don't teach her the lower case or 'small' **a** at this time, nor refer to the already learned letter **C**. When, and only when, she can associate the correct sound with the symbol **A**, and can detect the *a* sound at the beginning of words, and can pick out the **A**s in printed text, is she ready for the next step.

Having learned two letters now, Emerald is apt to confuse them, so she needs practice in distinguishing between the two. A game fills this need well; moreover, it will entertain her until that time when the content of the text itself serves to entertain.

The Egg Carton Game

The best teaching games for young children combine a minimum of logic and a maximum of repetition and nonsense. The following game fills that description. To construct the game all you need are a hundred blank business cards obtainable at a stationers (or use the backs of any old business cards you may have), two dozen pennies (or marbles or poker chips if you prefer), an egg carton, six bottle caps, and a wide felt-tip marker.

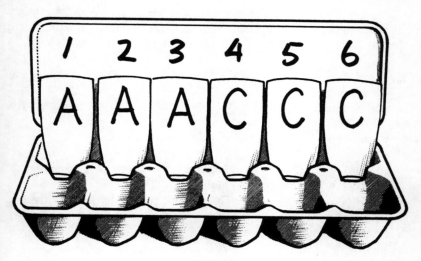

Figure 4: *The egg carton game.*

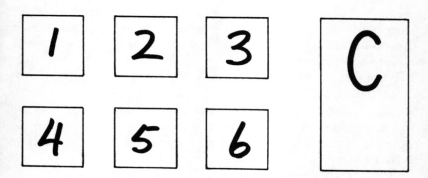

Figure 5: *Cards with different numbers*

Figure 6: *The letters on larger cards.*

Cut three business cards in half. Print numbers 1 to 6 on the halves as has been done in Figure 5. Mix the cards and place them face down in a soup bowl. Print the numbers 1 to 6 inside the lid of the egg carton as has been done in Figure 4. If you aren't confident about printing numbers accurately, cut numbers from a calendar and glue them in place.

Print the letter **C** on three business cards in the manner shown in Figure 6, and the letter **A** on three others. Bend the cards slightly at their bottoms and insert them in the back row of the egg carton, as seen in Figure 4.

Because the counters – which can be coins, marbles, or poker chips – are to be handled in the presence of food, they might be cleaned in bleach before beginning the game. While playing, the counters will be deposited in various cups of the egg carton. Children like things that rattle or clatter, so place a bottle cap – metal side up – in the bottom of each cup of the carton – 12 in all. Now each coin, when deposited, will issue a reassuring click.

Before showing Emerald the game, review the letters **C** and **A** separately. That done, place something – a jar, perhaps – behind the egg carton to hold the lid upright.

It doesn't matter whether or not Emerald can count to six or whether she knows the symbols that represent these amounts, as far as she is concerned she will merely be matching symbols while playing the game. Instead of using numbers, you might use duplicate heads of comic characters, or photos of members of the family or different colored papers. Or if you would like to familiarize Emerald with geometric shapes you could use symbols: star, circle, square, rectangle, oval, and triangle.

To begin play, have Emerald take a card from the soup bowl, then find the same symbol (or number) inside the lid of the egg carton. Have her deposit a counter (coin, marble or poker chip) in the *front* cup that lines up with the number marked on the lid, and sound the letter printed on the card in the rear cup. The numbered card she drew from the bowl is then placed to one side. She then draws another card from the bowl, finds its matching symbol on the lid of the egg carton, deposits a counter in the appropriate *front* cup, and sounds the letter in the rear cup.

The game continues in this way until a counter has been placed in each of the six front cups. Emerald then puts the six numbered cards back in the soup bowl, face down, and, draws them again one by one, placing counters – this time – in the *back* cups, and sounds the appropriate letter. This time, though, Emerald removes the letter-card from the rear cup when she deposits the counter. When all six of the letter cards have been removed, the game is over.

It might occur to you that Emerald could as easily have placed counters in the twelve cups without drawing any numbered cards for direction. True. The point is, though, that the procedure *looks* important to the child – important 'business' as it were – and makes her feel important because she is creating the chance order of events.

Accept the six cards from Emerald as payment for a treat – which may take the form of six raisins, or peanuts, or corn flakes, or something else, but always choose a food item that wouldn't normally be part of a meal. Or you might accept the six cards as payment for some treat to be eaten after supper. Or the item 'earned' might be something other than food: a paper figure or doll from a press-out book.

The Question of Rewards

The use of rewards is sometimes questioned, so a word on this practice might be appropriate. Some believe that giving children rewards is unnecessary, perhaps even degrading, as if one were training an animal. Whether rewards are degrading must remain a matter of opinion. But the *necessity* of rewards is a different matter. Those parents fortunate enough to have teaching experience, or who have a knack for fascinating children and turning their attention this way or that, may not need to use rewards. From my own observation, though, rewards are indispensable in the education of children by parents who are pinched for time and lack special teaching skill.

Frankly, questioning the use of rewards smacks of hypocrisy. What human endeavor is not dominated by thoughts of reward? Soldiers value medals, actors value acclaim, salespeople value money – with self-satisfaction added to all three. I have always regarded the practice of forcing schoolchildren to learn matters that do not interest them – and to do so without payment – as an indefensible form of mental cruelty. How I loathed the study of history before I attained an age (adulthood) when it became interesting.

There are, unquestionably, teaching situations where extrinsic or external rewards are neither necessary nor desirable, where, in fact, payment of a reward would condition the learner to devalue the intrinsic pleasure of the activity. But there are, with equal certainty, other situations where quick, pleasant learning will not be achieved without the use of extrinsic reward; particularly in the acquisition of 'tool' skills such as reading, writing, and arithmetic. With each of these skills, the learner is required to pass through an initial period when there is little inherent pleasure in the activity. Reading, when it is well taught, has probably the shortest such period. Teachers in the junior rooms at the Institute find a comic face rubber-stamped on the backs of children's hands provides an adequate reward, or for variation, a small self-adhering stamp.

The use of rewards here plays an important role while children are gaining skill with the brute mechanics of reading. Gradually, as reading becomes easier and children begin to enjoy the material they read, rewards are discontinued and the content of each book becomes its own reward.

The Dunce Puppet

The Reading Game or School Game – whichever you choose to call it – becomes more entertaining and exciting if you introduce a puppet to the game. Children love to crow over the mistakes of an apparently silly person (which explains the success of several famous comedians). By giving voice to the puppet and letting him have a turn at the game, he can appear to perform all manner of outrageous errors that will captivate your child – let's call him Cosgrove – and maintain high excitement throughout the game. If the puppet is made to fill the role of braggart – presuming to know everything while making absurd blunders – Cosgrove will become emotionally caught up in the Reading Game, and he'll clamor to play the game as soon as he sits at the table. The puppet can thereafter be made to fill the role of pupil, and Cosgrove, now a teacher, can teach the puppet to read. Use of rewards and the puppet will make your reading program so delightful that playing the game can be made a reward in itself; perhaps one that is dependent upon the fulfillment of some other condition: "Finish your cabbage, Cosgrove, then we'll play the Reading Game."

Figure 7: *The dunce puppet is a useful and entertaining teaching tool.*

Parents may ask, "How do you work the puppet?" It takes just a little nerve and a little practice. If your hand puppet is of the sort that permits you to open and close the mouth, fine. You may find, though, that the natural tendency is to close your hand (and the puppet's mouth) when it should be opening. Practice reversing this natural inclination until you can do it easily. Even a puppet with a fixed mouth – or just a teddy bear or some other stuffed animal – can fascinate a child. Children tend to see what they want to see (adults too, perhaps?), so you need only provide a silly voice and sputter out a line of chatter to hold the child's attention. Be sure to look at the puppet when it's 'talking', thus directing your child's eyes to the puppet and adding to the impression that it is the puppet speaking, and not you.

When your child can easily distinguish between **A** and **C**, and can make the appropriate sound for each, the letter **T** can be brought into the game. However, several days before you introduce the letter **T** – or any other new letter – engage your youngster in the practice of detecting that sound at the beginning of words; in this case words such as *truck, tire, train, taxi, tap, table, television, toy,* and *tongue.* Show your child the **T** on page 61 and have him trace its shape with his finger while making the appropriate sound – sounded *not* as 'tee', but as a voiceless rush of air as the tongue leaves the roof of the mouth. Then help him find **T**s in the newspaper headlines. Finally, print **T** on two business cards and substitute these in the game for one **A** and one **C**. The six cards in the game will now be two **A**s, two **C**s, and two **T**s.

When the material used in the egg carton game is well known to your child and you no longer have to watch and correct him, the game might be taken along in the car. With the game sitting on the child's lap, perhaps on a TV tray, he will be able to play a couple of games while you drive.

Reading Words

When Cosgrove can quickly and easily distinguish between the letters **C**, **A**, and **T**, he is ready to read his first word, *cat.* Print **CAT** on two business cards and use these in the game along with one **A**, one **C**, and two **T**s.

Don't expect him to immediately see that the blended sounds of **C**, **A**, and **T** compose the name of a familiar animal. Even though you point out this obvious fact (obvious only to you and me) he may fail to see the connection. Don't make a big issue of his puzzlement. The information will eventually click into place on its own.

Cosgrove will need plenty of practice in the ritual of left-to-right-information-gathering before he can easily identify the sound symbols

70

in *cat* in a left-to-right order, and not in a right-to-left order. To a child, there is no logic in the prescribed one-way-only direction for reading so don't expect him to become accustomed to a left-to-right decoding ritual until he has practiced the procedure a few hundred times. Even then, he may have occasional lapses and read backwards. Such errors are normal.

One way to encourage left-to-right reading is to cut out and glue the head of a comic character on the left side of the card (Figure 8). Asked what the funny figure is saying, the child is likely to begin sounding letters nearest the comic head first. Even better, use a photo of Cosgrove.

Figure 8: *Cartoon characters placed on the top left corner of cards help children remember to read from left to right.*

Make certain Cosgrove sounds each letter in **CAT** before speaking the entire word. At this time, we are not so much interested in his learning to read a particular word as learning a sounding-out procedure that will soon permit him to puzzle out all words for himself, words he has never seen in print before. Therefore, don't discourage the youngster from sounding each letter in a word before reading the entire word. His voiced procedure then, would be "Kuh, a, tuh – cat," but with the *uh* in 'kuh' and *uh* in 'tuh' representing only an escape of air and lacking voice.

An important rule to observe – and one that hastens learning – is to never introduce new material to the game while your child is still unsure of material already presented. So important is this rule, and so susceptible is the rule to parental oversight, that it deserves repeating: *Never introduce new material to the game while your child is still unsure of material already presented.*

When Cosgrove is easily able to deal with the letters **C**, **A**, and **T**, and the word **CAT**, introduce the letter **P**, sounded *not* as 'pea', but simply as an unvoiced expulsion of air as your lips part – as if you were blowing out a candle but not trying very hard. The steps to follow with the letter **P** are those already used for the letters **C**, **A**, and **T**, and are the same steps to be used for introducing each successive letter. Here they are.

1. Help him detect the sound of the letter in words that begin with that letter.
2. Have him trace his finger around the shape of the appropriate letter on pages 61-63 while making the correct sound.
3. Help him to find the letter in printed text – in newspaper headlines, perhaps – and sound the letter properly each time.

How many times will he have to play the game to learn the material well? There's no knowing. Children progress at different speeds. Proceed *slowly*. Parents sometimes make the mistake of introducing new letters and words too quickly. Don't rush. Just because your youngster seems to know the material today doesn't mean he will know it tomorrow, and if his lapse of memory is coupled with the learning of new material, his confusion will be increased and quick advancement will be doomed. Give extra time to any material that seems to confuse him.

Children, like adults, don't enjoy activities that make them look dumb. If Cosgrove's enthusiasm seems to drop, it may be because he is unsure of the material. In this case, back off. Buoy up his self-confidence by bringing back into the game material he knows well. You aren't likely to bore the youngster with old material. Children rarely become bored with being *correct*, especially when it wins them rewards and fun with the silly puppet.

After learning the letter **P**, Cosgrove will be able to read two new words: *cap* and *tap*. But don't – now, or at any time – introduce *two* new items to the game at the same time. By observing this important rule you will help guarantee his quick progress. If he doesn't know that a cap is a type of hat, show him one, or show him a picture of someone wearing a cap. Similarly, if there are any other words in Figure 9 that your child doesn't know – for example *wig, van, vessel, fizz* – explain their meaning to him long before they are included in the game.

Print **CAP** on two cards and include them in the egg carton game along with **CAT** on two cards and **T** on two others. When, after several games, he is completely at ease with this material, print **TAP** on two cards and substitute these for the two **T** cards.

Figure 9 shows the letters and words that have been learned to this point (down to position 4), and the order in which new letters and new words should be included in the game.

Row A, in Figure 10, shows the six cards as they will now appear in the game. In Row B, two cards – Pair 1 – have been replaced with two new cards bearing **N**. In Row C, these have been replaced with cards bearing two words. In Row D, and in each successive row through to Row K, two more cards have been replaced.

Row K shows the cards in the game as the material at position 8 in Figure 9 is about to be introduced. The small circled numbers in Figure 10 show the order in which the pairs of cards are changed. Follow this same progression, 1 through 9 when you introduce the rest of the material in Figure 9.

Teach your daughter, Freda, to sound each new letter as it is sounded in the new words. Notice that the following letters are *not* accompanied by a voiced sound: **S**, **H**, **F**, **K**, **X**. Regrettably, **X** must be sounded as it does at the *end* of a word – *ks* – like the word *kiss* with the *i* left out. Be careful not to add a grunted *uh* when you sound **N, M, L, R, W, V, Y**. Each is just a steady tone that can be sounded as long as you wish. (**Y** is *ee*). The letters **B**, **G**, **D**, **J** are different in that the voiced sound is abruptly halted as soon as the tongue or lips complete their movement. If you give a sound 'tail' to **B**, for example – as buh-h-h – Freda will have a poor understanding of the correct sound.

The four remaining vowels are pure voiced sounds. **E** is given the sound heard in *pen*, but drawn out: *eh-h-h*. **U** is sounded as in *cup*: *uh-h-h*, **I** as heard in *tin*, and **O** as in *hot*. Each such sound can be drawn out or extended.

If, while learning the material down to position 27 on Figure 9, Freda prefers to occasionally read words without sounding the individual letters, fine, but *don't* coach her to do so.

If she wonders why two **S**s or two **F**s or two **Z**s are used (in *kiss, vessel, puff,* and *fizz*) when just one of each letter would seem enough, just tell her that's the way it is. But you will need to point out that two **E**s and two **O**s (as in *queen* and *zoo*) combine to form a new sound. Explain the **CK** combination in *quick* briefly. Just say the **C** sound

	NEW LETTERS	NEW WORDS		NEW LETTERS	NEW WORDS
1	C		14	G	GUM PIG
2	A		15	L	LEG PAL
3	T	CAT	16	R	RUG CRIB
4	P	CAP TAP	17	D	DROP GLAD
			18	F	FROG PUFF
5	N	CAN PAN	19	K	KISS SINK
6	E	PEN NET	20	W	WING WIG
7	U	CUP NUT	21	V	VAN VESSEL
8	I	TIN PIN	22	J	JUG JUMP
9	O	TOP POT	23	X	FOX FIX
10	S	SIT NUTS	24	Y	YES YOU
11	B	BAT TUB	25	Z	ZOO FIZZ
12	H	HOT HEN	26	QU	QUICK QUEEN
13	M	MOP MAN	27	TH	THIS THAT

Figure 9

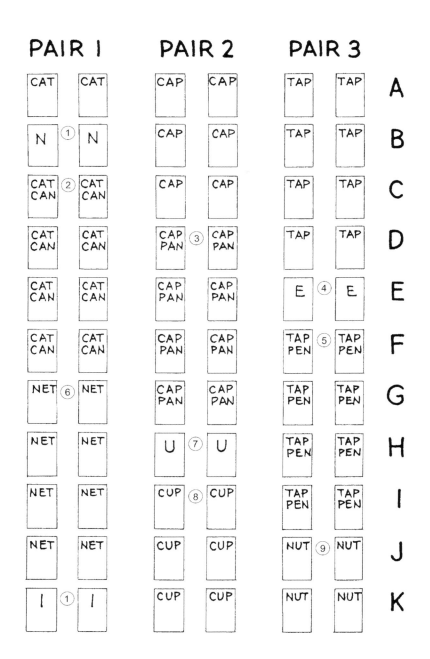

PAIR 1 PAIR 2 PAIR 3

	PAIR 1		PAIR 2		PAIR 3		
A	CAT	CAT	CAP	CAP	TAP	TAP	
B	N	N	CAP	CAP	TAP	TAP	
C	CAT CAN	CAT CAN	CAP	CAP	TAP	TAP	
D	CAT CAN	CAT CAN	CAP PAN	CAP PAN	TAP	TAP	
E	CAT CAN	CAT CAN	CAP PAN	CAP PAN	E	E	
F	CAT CAN	CAT CAN	CAP PAN	CAP PAN	TAP PEN	TAP PEN	
G	NET	NET	CAP PAN	CAP PAN	TAP PEN	TAP PEN	
H	NET	NET	U	U	TAP PEN	TAP PEN	
I	NET	NET	CUP	CUP	TAP PEN	TAP PEN	
J	NET	NET	CUP	CUP	NUT	NUT	
K	I	I	CUP	CUP	NUT	NUT	

Figure 10

75

sometimes takes the form of **CK**. Freda need not sound the individual letters in *you*, one of the irregular words in our language.

When cards bearing two words have been removed from the game, they should be returned to the game periodically for review. Children have a short memory for newly learned material.

How quickly will Freda learn the material down to Row 27? That depends on how often she plays the game and how well you teach the letter sounds. If she plays one or two games at suppertime and a few games each week with tutors, her speed of progress may surprise you. Repetition is the accelerator. The more often the child plays the game, the more quickly will she progress.

Freda may sometimes surprise you by claiming she has never seen a word before, even though she has read the word dozens of times. Or she may suddenly begin having difficulty with a word after having read it correctly a hundred or so times. And you may also be amazed to see her reading – with apparent unconcern – upside-down, or even sideways. The truth is that children sometimes possess astonishing skill for reading in an unconventional manner, so they see little reason for not doing so. Such deviations are, within limits, completely normal. But if your youngster's progress ever stops, or if she seems to have continuing difficulty in isolating speech sounds, you might have her hearing tested. Similarly, if she has continuing difficulty in distinguishing between smaller versions of letters, you might have her vision tested.

Reading Bingo

When Freda has learned the material in Figure 9 down to **BAT** (Row 11) you will then be able to engage her in a new educating pastime while driving. Photocopy the grid shown at Figure 11, and play Reading Bingo. You could keep a list of the sixteen words on the dashboard and call them out at random. With the grid set on a tray on her lap, and with a small bowl of peanuts (split in two to avoid rolling) or raisins, Freda would place an edible item on each word you call out. When she has formed a line in any direction, she would eat the markers – either those in the winning line or all the markers on the grid. You can alter the winning pattern in any way you choose; Freda might be obliged to fill *two* lines, or perhaps the four corner squares.

To imbed the letter sounds more firmly in Freda's mind, you might sound out the letters before you voice the word: to illustrate, "N-n-n, eh-h-h, tuh – *net*." And to make sure she places a marker on the correct square (without taking your eyes off the road), have her sound out the letters of each word she places a marker on.

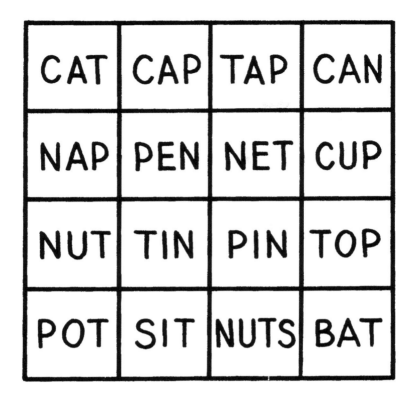

Figure 11: *The Reading Bingo game.*

You could as easily play the game at home before supper; thus keeping her occupied while you prepare the meal. Letter each new word Freda learns on a piece of paper and glue it on the grid to replace some other word she knows well.

As new letters are learned, many more words could be included in the game than those few shown in Figure 9. But adding words to the program might slow a child's progress. Our purpose here is to quickly give the youngster use of the letter-sound code: a skill that will then permit her to pry open the contents of unknown words much in the way a can-opener would let her discover the contents of unlabeled cans of food. As Freda gains skill in using the letter code, she will gradually stop sounding individual letters in a word before reading it. She will instead begin to mentally sound the letters she has been voicing.

When Pembroke has learned the material down to Row 27, you can begin to teach him the lower-case or 'small' letters. The method we will

A QUICK BROWN FOX JUMPS OVER THE LAZY DOG

b - 1 A QUICK bROWN FOX JUMPS OVER THE LAZY DOG

e - 2 A QUICK bROWN FOX JUMPS OVeR THe LAZY DOG

a - 3 a QUICK bROWN FOX JUMPS OVeR THe LaZY DOG

n - 4 a QUICK bROWn FOX JUMPS OVeR THe LaZY DOG

r - 5 a QUICK brOWn FOX JUMPS OVer THe LaZY DOG

g - 6 a QUICK brOWn FOX JUMPS OVer THe Lazy Dog

i - 7 a QUiCK brown FOX JUMPS over THe Lazy Dog

f - 8   a QUiCK brown fox JUMPS over THe Lazy Dog

j - 9   a QUiCK brown fox jUMPS over THe Lazy Dog

q - 10   a quiCK brown fox jUMPS over THe Lazy Dog

m - 11   a quiCK brown fox jumPS over THe Lazy Dog

t - 12   a quick brown fox jumPS over tHe Lazy Dog

l - 13   a quick brown fox jumps over tHe lazy Dog

d - 14   a quick brown fox jumps over tHe lazy dog

h - 15   a quick brown fox jumps over the lazy dog

use reduces confusion to a minimum. The letters *p, q, b,* and *d*, are of particular concern because they have always puzzled children. Begin by helping him read the top sentence on page 78.

You will need to tell Pembroke that **O** and **W** sometimes combine to give us the sound in *brown* (sometimes they don't, as in *show*). He may be surprised to find a different sound being given to **O** in *over*. Just explain that the letters sometimes stands for this sound too. The **ER** combination in *over* should receive just a brief explanation, as should the pronunciation of **E** in *the*.

That's the Way It Is

Parents shouldn't feel personally accountable for the irregularities of our language. Those irregularities than can be easily explained should be explained; those that can't should be treated with a matter-of-fact "That's the way it is." Keep rules to a minimum, and leave yourself a loophole by saying this or that letter 'usually' or 'often', or 'sometimes' sounds in such-and-such a way (depending on which of these words is suitable and is understood by your child). For example, saying that the letters *C* and *H always* represent the sound heard in *church* is proved wrong in the word *school*.

When Pembroke can read the 'quick brown fox' sentence easily, explain to him that there is another way the **B** sound can be shown. Show him the lower case **b** in the second line on page 78, then let him read Sentence 1 a couple of times. The next day, explain that the letter **E** can appear differently. Show him this new letterform and let him read Sentence 2 a few times. Continue in this way, explaining a new letterform each day and let him read the next sentence.

Motivation

If a child loses interest in the reading program, the parent may be trying to advance too quickly or has failed to make the program a fun-filled procedure with occasional laughs. A parent might even be tempted to coax the child to engage in the exercise. Better not. Take a break from the program or turn it over to one or more tutors.

Edible rewards would hold little attraction for children during mealtime reading sessions, but they can be a great help to the tutors at other times. Most important, a child's basic nutritional requirement must never be conditional upon engaging in an educational activity. If tutors teach before supper, the treats will have to be kept small so they don't upset the child's appetite. Junk food – candy, potato chips, popcorn, corn puffs, sugared cereals, and similar fare – aren't recommended before a meal. If the child's appetite is going to be diminished by pre-supper treats, let them be wholesome foods: peanuts, circles of banana topped with a small dab of peanut butter, or small sections of other fruits.

If tutors teach after supper, sweet foods, and perhaps even some junk food, might be included in the treats before tooth brushing. The suitability of this or that food item for use as a reward will be determined by circumstance. A youngster who eats candy and pastry every day may not be too excited about getting a few peanuts. Also, a five-year-old has different reward preferences than a two-year-old.

A youngster of four or five may welcome a store-in-the-home arrangement that has proved popular with other children of that age. Take the child out shopping and buy a few small items he would like to work for: gummed stickers of birds or animals, press-out books of dolls and doll clothes, plastic jewelry, model cars and such. These items might then be displayed prominently in the dining area or even attached with clothespins to a line strung up expressly for that purpose. Each time the reading game is played, the child would be credited with a certain amount of money toward the purchase of a particular item of his choice. The youngster might, in fact, be allowed to keep the twelve pennies used in the egg-carton game as savings toward the desired item. You may find that when Pembroke finally earns a desired toy, he will treasure it more than if he had received it as a gift.

Reading Books

Pembroke, now knowing the upper-case and lower-case letters and having a good basic understanding of the letter-sound code, can now begin learning how other letter combinations – *or, ur, sh, ph,* and so on – are sounded: information that can be gained while reading simple books. A child's first books should be purchased rather than borrowed for two reasons: first, parents will then be able to turn the books into reading-instruction texts by adding words to each page, and second, a youngster will enjoy reading these same books again, months, perhaps even years, later.

Buy books that have the following features: large print, just one or two sentences per page, and space for you to print in words of your own. Your reading procedure will vary with the books selected, but for purposes of illustration, let's suppose the first page of a book contains the sentence: *Two children named Harvey and Gertrude lived near a large forest.* If Pembroke doesn't know the meaning of *forest,* and an illustration isn't shown in the book, explain to him what a forest is, and find a picture somewhere of a forest. Next, explain any new letter combination in the sentence. The word *two* can't be explained logically. Just tell him it's a word that doesn't sound the way it looks and let the matter go at that. In *children*, he encounters the **CH** combination for the first time. Teach him a couple of words that contain this same combination – perhaps *cheese* and *lunch* – and print these words on the page of the book. In words such as *named*, where the letter **a** is pronounced differently from the way he learned to sound it, simply point out the change needed without getting involved with rules of pronunciation (E at the end of a word …) And when a letter is not pronounced, as in the case of **e** in *named*, mention this too. "In this word, Pembroke, we say *ay* instead of *a*, and we don't sound the *eh-h*." In the name *Harvey*, he encounters the **AR** combination, so you could introduce him to the words *car* and *farm* and print these on the page.

Continuing in this way, a simple reading book can be turned into a valuable textbook for your child. As you progress through its pages, you will have less occasion to insert words because there will be fewer letter combinations Pembroke hasn't already encountered. Include in the egg-carton game any word he has difficulty with. When he stumbles over a word, *don't read it for him*. Instead, encourage him to sound out the letters and identify the word for himself. If he guesses at a word, point out to him that he is merely guessing. Make a few wild guesses yourself and have a laugh. Then help him to sound out the letters. Sometimes you may be surprised at the number of words he is able to puzzle out without your help. For example, in sounding the letters in *was*, an unknown word *wass* (rhyming with *pass*) would seem to be indicated, but the child may then alter the sound and, after reading the word a few times, will automatically supply the correct sound. Children have been seen to puzzle out, without help, the words *someone, nose, ear*, and *water*. You may find Pembroke doing the same.

A common mistake parents make when their children begin reading is to try to hurry them into thicker books. Resist the urge. Choose simple books; ones with no more than a couple of hundred words.

Don't discourage Pembroke from reading aloud. Only by having him read aloud can you tell if he is having difficulties with his reading. Similarly, don't discourage him from running his finger along beneath words. He will discontinue this practice on his own when he no longer finds it reassuring.

When Pembroke has read his first dozen books or so, he will be ready for the final procedure that turns a beginning reader into a lover of books, and that is the subject of the next chapter.

Encouraging the Habit of Reading

Teaching your child – let's call her Amethyst – to read doesn't guarantee she will become a skillful reader. Nor does it guarantee that reading will ever play an important part in her life. For example, a child who has been taught to read but is then allowed to watch unlimited television may not choose books for her entertainment. And the child who reads seldom is not likely to read well, so, lacking speed and ease in reading, she will tend to avoid reading. In this way, a pattern is established that thwarts any advancement in reading.

The role of television in children's lives is discussed in Chapter 14. For the moment though, while we are concerned with improving children's reading, television will be considered, at worst, a negative influence and, at best, a weak teaching ally. Briefly, the effectiveness of procedures described here may be diminished by the extent to which Amethyst watches television.

Reading Comprehension

A child will understand in printed form those words, and only those words, he or she understands in spoken form. But understanding *whole groups* of words that describe a specific situation poses a different problem. We might liken the difficulty faced by a beginning reader to that faced by a beginning driver of an automobile. The beginning driver must remember many things. He must be careful of his speed, must steer carefully, must watch other cars, pedestrians, traffic signs and lights, and be ready to release the accelerator and apply the brake quickly. All very simple, of course, for an experienced driver, but nerve tingling for a beginner.

If, after completing a white-knuckle drive around the block, the learner were asked by the instructor if he'd noticed the large beautiful dog tied up under the apple tree beside the white cottage, the instructor would be thought mad. The beginning driver couldn't divide his attention between driving and admiring the scenery. He's happy just to get around the block without an accident. Only the skillful driver can pay attention to the scenery.

Similarly, the beginning reader – concentrating as he is on reading from left to right, then remembering to drop down one line, careful, not two lines, and begin reading again from left to right, applying a particular letter-sound rule to this word, then, perhaps a different rule to some other word – can become so absorbed with the mechanics of reading that he fails to notice the 'scenery': that the story is about a large beautiful dog tied up under an apple tree beside a white cottage.

This may explain why parents of beginning readers sometimes say, "Yes, she can read, but she doesn't seem to understand, or even remember, what she reads." Not surprisingly! The beginner is too busy processing a train of individual words to be able to sweep them together quickly and form a picture of what the author had in mind. Furthermore, if a child reads so slowly that, by the time she has worked her way laboriously through to the end of a sentence she has forgotten how the sentence began, she cannot properly understand what she reads.

When a child's reading becomes quick and sure, she will then – like the skillful driver – be able to notice the scenery. Comprehension in reading, as we now see, is dependent not only upon skillful use of the letter-sound code and possession of a working vocabulary, but also on the speed and ease (speed-reading not intended) with which a child can process lines of text. Facility in reading is, therefore, a requisite for understanding what is read. And because the speed with which a child reads is dependent upon how much and how often she reads, a child should be encouraged to read often. The child in question might be a two- or three-year-old who is now reading simple books or she might be a teenager who rarely reads; one who may, in fact, read little better than the preschooler. Let's consider ways we might improve the reading ability for children of all ages.

Blueprint for a Bibliophile

There is a surefire way to turn a child away from reading, and that is to oblige the youngster to read books he finds difficult. Parents will wisely resist the urge to lure youngsters into reading advanced material. Granted, you want him or her to advance, and the sooner the better. But pressing for a quick advancement can jeopardize a child's love of reading. By reading easy books, children grow to love books. Better that a child read twenty simple books of his own choosing each week than a few difficult books selected by parents.

Someone has said there are three ways to get something done: do it yourself, or hire someone to do it, or forbid your children to do it. There is no denying that children's interest in any venture soars when apparent limits or restraints are imposed. This holds true for reading too. One tactic that effectively increased interest in reading for three- and four-year-olds was to appear unenthusiastic about lengthening their reading time in bed each night. A flimsy objection was usually voiced to deter further reading – the lateness of the hour, the fact they'd already read one or two books. But, of course, 'reluctant' approval was always given for a third, fourth, and even a fifth book.

You may perceive a risk in letting children think they can alter a parental preference, but the risk will exist only in homes where parents are habitually undecided or weak in their resolve; which is different when children know that extended reading is the only activity open to negotiation.

At other times, some easily surmountable obstacle might thwart a child's reading, thereby raising reading to the level of a reward. For example, a mild objection might be raised that clothes were scattered on the floor or toys left untidy; this, prompting a small amount of industry for the child to win the right to read.

Presuming Amethyst watches TV occasionally, she might be motivated to read books dealing with the subject viewed. The public library presents the greatest single source of fascinating reading with books on a variety of intriguing subjects such as space exploration, mysteries of the sea, strange creatures, unusual people, and so on. Many interesting topics are written in a simplified form. Ask the librarian to explain how the children's section is set up, then spend some time acquainting yourself with the contents of the various shelves.

Series Books

When Amethyst has read a few hundred books (not necessarily *different* books, for she might read some books several times), and her vocabulary has grown, she will begin to show interest in longer books. Such books will help to enlarge her vocabulary even more. However, our purpose in teaching children to read shouldn't be to fill their life solely with learning. Fiction has a role to play too. The librarian at your public library will tell you which fictional works are popular at your child's reading level. Series books (sets of books having the same heroes or heroines) are a good choice. They wouldn't have grown into a series if the author hadn't proved she could fascinate children. Perhaps you, yourself, enjoyed the adventures of Nancy Drew, the Bobbsey twins or Enid Blyton's books from England. Other books have now replaced those engaging classics: the *Magic Tree House* for younger children, the Harry Potter series and the *Series of Unfortunate Events* for older children.

Don't expect Amethyst to graduate to the series books quickly. Thick books (and series books tend to be thick) can discourage children if they aren't reading quickly and effortlessly. A child may read for two or three years before she will tackle books of 25,000 words in length, and another year or two may pass before she wants to read books of 60,000 words or more.

Because children love to read the same book more than once, you may wish to buy your own copies. One way to keep costs down is to buy secondhand books. By purchasing books instead of borrowing them, you provide a handy, constantly tempting source of entertainment for your child – an alternative source of entertainment to television.

> ### Precise Speech
> By having your child read aloud from books, you or the tutors could make the readings serve as an exercise in diction, every final *d, t,* and *ing* to be clearly enunciated.

The Schoolchild

If Amethyst is already in school but hasn't yet learned to use the letter-sound code easily, take her through the reading program described in Chapter 7. How can you tell if she can't use the code easily? Have her read the text below. A child who has been correctly taught the letter code and has been practiced in using the code will find the text easy to read.

cuff   frost   blink   plump   bud
RON FED HIS PET RAT A YAM
JAN SAW A TIN OF WAX IN
THE HUT

Figure 13 – *A literacy test*

Will your home reading program conflict with what is being taught at your local school? That depends on *what* is being taught in school. Slow, faulty reading programs can still be found in some schools. The most disastrous reading program of all time (Dick and Jane) was finally removed from classrooms after having created an incalculable number of functional illiterates and unenthusiastic readers. And no wonder! The teachers' handbooks contained the following advice:

> *Avoid having the children pronounce the phonetic* [letter-sound] *elements separately. Blending is done mentally, not vocally. Words should be pronounced as wholes in order that the appropriate sound and the natural blend of the elements will be produced clearly but not distorted.*

It sounds impressive and authoritative, like words from heaven telling teachers the divinely contrived secret for quick reading advancement. But, noticing the crippling influence this practice imposed on children's reading progress, many teachers ignored the advice and engaged in an illicit practice that became known as 'bootleg phonics' – they taught children to voice the sounds of the letters.

Why did it take so many years for administrators to discover the failings of Dick and Jane? Because some children managed to learn to read even when they were obliged to respect the phonics-hobbling rule. Other children stumbled on with near-success. Some, however, couldn't puzzle out how to blend letters by the prescribed 'in the head' method. These children progressed slowly and haltingly, grew discouraged and lost interest in reading as each month, each term, and each year passed. They were labeled dyslexic or learning disadvantaged and remained illiterate.

How did school administrators explain these failures to parents? Blame was diverted to the stresses and disadvantages in children's lives that supposedly prevented easy learning: sibling rivalry, too much TV, unsettled home life (parents fought, used drugs or were alcoholics). I mention this caper only because those who promote this sort of thinking are alive and well today, hold lofty positions in education, and continue to misdirect teachers and parents.

If your child can read the text in Figure 13, fine. Your job is simple. Improve his reading by the methods presented here.

Will your child's teacher mind? His teacher should be delighted. After all, you will be demonstrating the initiative and support teachers cry for. And looking at it another way, every child who can read well at the end of Grade 1 or 2 – whether success is due to the teacher or to parents – is scored as a success by the teacher and by the school.

The Comic Kingdom

Children love comic books, but the violence in some comic books is excessive. Parents might rightly regard this form of literature with apprehension if, in fact, the books can even be regarded as literature. However, the literary worth of comic books isn't our concern here. We are interested in skillful reading, not aesthetics, and to whatever extent comic books can provoke youngsters to use their reading ability, comic books will be considered valuable.

Not *all* comic books are unsavory. By glancing through comic books before purchasing them, you can weed out the unsuitable ones. A number of books featuring Disney characters provide savory reading for all ages, while the series featuring the *Simpsons* and *Archie* enthrall older children. Your telephone book may list dealers in comic books.

Magazines

Children's magazines contain highly entertaining material. Indeed, it's a matter of survival that they do so. Children won't tolerate dull writing. By subscribing to children's magazines you enlist the help of top-flight writers and editors to fasten your child's thoughts on reading. A wealth of excellent periodicals can be found by typing *children's magazines* into an internet search engine. Also, check the selection to be found at the public library. Borrow a few issues; see which of them catches your child's interest, then subscribe to one or more.

Reading while eating is considered bad manners. If you tried to sneak a book onto the table at, say, Buckingham Palace, you might not be asked back. However, it's a peccadillo common to many. Whether or not reading at the table is appropriate in your home is a matter for you to decide. But if mealtime conversation flounders or seems to dwell on unimportant trivia, you might be better off seeking diversion in printed form. Mealtime etiquette might therefore be safely bent and any of the books or publications that have been mentioned could be propped up and read aloud during meals. If your child is a skillful reader, he or she might be permitted to take a turn reading. Bookstands that hold books upright for easy reading are available at stationery stores.

Encyclopedias

An encyclopedia affords almost limitless fascinating reading. No family should be without an encyclopedia, nor need they be. Both new and used encyclopedias can be found by typing *encyclopedia* into an internet search engine. A second-hand encyclopedia might be purchased for a fraction of its original cost. Most of the subjects that interest children will change little over a ten-year period so don't think you have to buy a new edition. Encyclopedias on compact discs are inexpensive, but pursuing an enquiry can be burdensome when you have to wait for the computer to boot up. Information is more quickly and easily found by flicking open a volume taken from the bookshelf.

Let Amethyst name a topic she'd like to know more about: how honey or peanut butter or ice cream is made; or details about elephants, tigers, or crocodiles; then bring the appropriate volume of your encyclopedia to the supper table for shared reading.

In one single-parent home, the child having the least amount of food left on her plate was permitted to read an entry in a children's encyclopedia until someone else caught up and took over the reading. A book on natural history sometimes replaced the encyclopedia, and fascinating details emerged on natural phenomena: how the immense tsunami waves are created; how quicksand pits are formed (and how to get out of one); why one type of wave (a bore) flows upstream instead of down, and other matters of interest to children and adults alike.

Each of these suggestions will encourage your child to read more, will improve her reading ability and will, in consequence, advance her knowledge and intelligence. And you may discover a bonus. You may find, as others have, that by playing a role in your child's education, you begin to fill gaps in your own.

Vocabulary Growth

The size of a child's vocabulary influences his intellectual and educational standing more than any other body of knowledge he possesses. Though other matters will be considered in the ensuing chapters, a parent who does no more than teach her child to read (Chapter 7), promote a love of reading (Chapter 8), and extend his vocabulary by the methods described in this chapter, will assure the child early brilliance and predispose him to academic success.

Why is the size and quality of a child's vocabulary so important? Because words are the working tools of thought. A child who has collected only a small set of these tools will have difficulty understanding other people's thoughts and expressing his own. Isn't the same true for adults? An adult who is limited to a small vocabulary is ill equipped to comprehend and discuss subjects at an advanced level.

Psychologists tell us the range of a child's vocabulary is one of the most stable and most reliable indicators of the child's intelligence from year to year. Children's IQ tests are divided into several parts, one of which measures the size and quality of vocabulary. Researchers have discovered that the score children achieve on the *vocabulary* portion of IQ tests is almost the same as their score on the entire test. In other words, for children at least, large vocabulary and high IQ are pretty much one and the same.

Should we really be surprised by this? Isn't this what the fathers of Bentham, Mill, and Witte believed, and proved, more than a hundred years ago? The intriguing part, however, is that enlarging children's vocabularies is *easy*. No expensive equipment is needed. No special training is required. Almost any parent can enlarge their child's vocabulary just by engaging their child in simple vocabulary-building activities. But the task isn't brief. Enlarging a child's vocabulary can span years. So, the material presented in this chapter to increase your child's vocabulary isn't to be completed before you move ahead with spelling, printing, and writing (dealt with next chapter). Instead, vocabulary growth is to be pursued along with those skills.

Words, Words, Words

For a child to enjoy storybooks, he must be able to understand the words used in the stories. Children will be able to understand, in *printed* form, only those words they can understand in *spoken* form. To illustrate: the sentence, *They jumped into the canoe and paddled away to the island*, is meaningless in either spoken or printed form to a child who doesn't know what a *canoe* is, or a *paddle*, or an *island*, and who doesn't understand the concept of *into*. Obviously, vocabulary is the window of perception: the larger the window the richer the understanding.

Seeing a word several times, and hearing it several times, helps children to learn words quickly; so, display each new word your youngster learns where he will see it often. Print a list, in large letters, of the new words and attach the list to the refrigerator or to the wall in the dining area. If the lists are attached in a way that permits their easy removal – as by magnets to the refrigerator – the lists can be taken along with you and clamped to the sun visor in the car.

	Introduce	Review
Day 1	Word 1	
Day 2	Word 2	Word 1
Day 3	Word 3	Word 1 & 2
Day 4	Word 4	Word 1,2,3
Day 5	Word 5	Word 1,2,3,4
Day 6	Word 6	Word 2,3,4,5
Day 7	Word 7	Word 3,4,5,6
Day 8	Word 8	Word 4,5,6,7
Day 9	Word 9	Word 5,6,7,8
Day 10	Review Words 1 to 9	
Day 11	Word 10	Word 6,7,8,9
Continue the sequence shown above with new words.		

Figure 14: *A procedure for learning new words.*

How quickly will your child's vocabulary grow? That depends on how you teach him. Attempting to teach a child many words in a short space of time will generally be slow and ineffectual. Your child, Everton, will merely confuse words or forget them. The chart above provides a sequence of steps that will help him remember each word you teach. Make your own blank chart and insert the words you intend to introduce.

Teach Everton a new word before breakfast – perhaps while dressing him. Pronounce the new word slowly, distinctly, and repeatedly, asking him to repeat the word each time. Use the new word several times in sentences. During breakfast, refresh his memory of the word, demonstrate the word, and have him voice the word again. Review the word in a similar way while driving to the daycare center. Review the word while driving home from the daycare in the afternoon and later during supper. Your reviews needn't be a production; a brief reminder is adequate. The magic element is repetition; that is, the number of times you encourage Everton to recall the information. If you trigger a brief remembrance of the word five or six times in the course of the day, he will have an easy use of it by bedtime. And he is likely to remember it.

The next day, following the procedure indicated in the chart, Figure 14, introduce a new word – Word 2 – and exercise Everton in its use as you did with the first word. Have him repeat the new word six or seven times. Equally important, review Word 1 a few times. Continue in the manner indicated by the chart, introducing a new word each day until the tenth day, which is given wholly to review, then, on the eleventh day introduce Word 10 and continue the sequence of introduction and review that has been established.

What words should you begin teaching? That depends on what words your child, Olga, already knows. Let's suppose we're dealing with a youngster who is only eighteen months old. If Olga benefited from the instruction given in Chapter 3 for a newborn child she will already have a good starting vocabulary, but let's suppose she missed this instruction and her vocabulary is about the same as that of most infants eighteen-months-old.

A ready first source of words is the child's body. Does she know the names given to the various parts of her body? If not, you will have a good supply of important words to begin with.

Words at Mealtime

Does Olga know the names of the various items at or near the supper table? Does she know what the pieces of cutlery are called, the various vessels, and receptacles? And what about the items seen from her seat at the table: *wire, wallpaper, keyhole, faucet (or tap) thermometer, hinge.* Place items on the dining table she might not know the names of: *toaster, egg cup, saucepan,* and *sieve.*

Food packaging provides its own special words: *ingredients, recipe, nourishing, flavor, servings, mixture, product, contents, directions, teaspoonful*. An assortment of objects kept in a bowl near the table might include any of the following for periodic inspection: *nut, bolt, screw, washer, nail, screwdriver, needle, candle, magnet, piece of string* or *thread*. Check cupboards and drawer to see what small items might be brought to the table, named, and explained. Even a handful of coins will permit you to teach the words *dull, shiny, round, copper, silver, nickel, click* (together), *roll* (on edge).

Employ surprise! Some item hidden beneath an overturned cup or bowl at breakfast is sure to delight her: *an eraser, a thimble, a clothespin, a thumbtack, a cork*. Show her how the object works and add its name to your word list. A touch of showmanship can add color to your program. "Well, Olga, just wait until you see what's under your cereal bowl this morning. No, I can't tell you because then it wouldn't be a surprise, would it? But just wait 'til you see it." Such a procedure might speed the dressing operation or brighten her early morning spirits if she tends to be grumpy. An elastic band or a paper clip many not seem very exciting to you, but to a child who is seeing them for the first time (or hearing the item named for the first time) and seeing how it works can be fascinating.

Don't forget to teach words that tell what objects are made of: *wood, metal, plastic, rubber, paper, leather, cloth, glass*, and show two or three object made of each. One of the new words taught each day might be some object she sees while driving. You could even take items along in the car for her to name during the trip.

Parents tend to forget what words children know or don't know, hence the added value of the charts you create for your vocabulary enrichment program.

Laughs are Important

Don't forget to be silly. Teaching new words each day and reviewing previously learned words shouldn't be a dreary procedure. What about testing the puppet's memory on some of the words? Have the puppet 'whisper' some stunningly ridiculous responses into your ear, to be conveyed to your pupil. (Use of the puppet is described on page 69.)

Words from Reading

Children enjoy hearing and reading stories that excite wonder, astonishment, or humor. Such stories can be used to teach new words in an entertaining manner, and in a way too that makes remembering them easier. Newspapers are a good source. Consider this actual report.

Is there a Santa Claus? According to the famous editorial response written in 1897 to eight-year-old Virginia O'Hanlon of New York; *"Yes, Virginia, there is a Santa Claus. He exists as certainly as love and generosity and devotion exist. Alas! How dreary would be the world if there were no Santa Claus!"*

Does Olga know the meaning of the words *famous, response, exist, certainly, generosity, devotion, alas, dreary* – and, depending on her age, *editorial*? The excerpt could be glued in a scrapbook entitled Newspaper Report Book.

Each time you see a report that might interest her – one that involves children, animals, strange and mysterious events – tell her just enough about the report to rouse her curiosity. She will then be tempted to read the entire article herself. Capitalize on objects pictured in newspapers and periodicals. "Look, Olga, see the bunch of flowers the lady's holding? It's called a bouquet."

The famous McGuffey Readers are credited with raising the vocabulary for children from immigrant families to a high level. Indeed, the Readers equipped children with a level of speech normally found in the homes of scholarly parents. The Readers, first published in 1836 (and still used in some schools today) contain words not common to the average child's vocabulary: words that are then explained at the end of each story. For example, an essay on the elephant in the Fourth Reader is followed by a definition of those words in the story that a nine-year-old reader might not know: *quadruped, pendulous, commerce, proboscis, stratagem, docile, asylum, unwieldy, tacitly, epidemic, nabob.* The Sixth Reader contains some of the best English prose ever written. The McGuffey Readers, rich with the themes of honesty, industry, kindness, consideration, and respect for others, though dated, fit well into a program of vocabulary growth.

Words while Driving

Your child, Baldwin, may already know the names of common objects seen while driving, such as *car, truck,* and *building.* Find out what words he doesn't know, perhaps *bridge, motorcycle, taxi* (or *cab*), and *license plate.* Gradually advance to less common words: *pedestrian, motorist, intersection, speedometer, high rise, skyscraper, underpass,* and *boulevard.*

A known word might lead to the introduction of an unknown word. "See that, Baldwin, that's called a bridge. You already knew it? Well, it's made of metal. You knew that too! Well, do you know where metal comes from? From a large hole people dig in the ground. Men go down into the hole to dig. It's called a mine, and the men who go into it are called miners." By such offshoot means the child will have learned *mine* and *miner*. You will naturally have to refresh his memory of the words a few times. If Baldwin is more advanced and you are teaching him to spell, in preparation for printing, spell each new word for him.

Another way to find new words while driving is by topic. Take speech, for example. What word do we normally connect with speech? *Talk, whisper, shout, holler, call, gossip.* Take another topic, music: *whistle, song, sing, singer, tune, melody, solo, duet, trio, quartet,* plus, perhaps the names of musical instruments he hears playing on the car radio.

Children are less likely to confuse words if the words indicate a wide variation in position or use. For example, you might introduce a word that refers to an object found in the home: *keyhole, oven, doorknob, picture, curtains, mirror.* The next word might then be an 'outside' word; something that is seen or has application mainly outside the home: *bark* of trees, *sidewalk, cloud, building, grass, sign, lamppost.*

The work of Dr. Francis H. Palmer at State University of New York at Stony Brook revealed that preschoolers who had been taught concepts indicating place, position, motion, and other qualities, scored as much as twenty-five points higher on IQ tests. These same youngsters also advanced more quickly in reading and mathematics: a lead they maintained throughout the upper grades. By testing three-year-olds across the country, Dr. Palmer learned how likely three-year-olds were to know these important concepts. Some of the words are shown on the next page along with the percentage of three-year-olds who knew each. See which ones your youngster knows and which ones he or she should be taught.

The Importance of Prepositions

Many of the concepts shown in Dr. Palmer's list are prepositions. In case you've forgotten, prepositions show the relationship of one item to another; for example, an object might be *in, out, between, under,* or *over* some other object. A child has seen people walk between things many times – between walls, between other people, between structures – but may still not have heard the word *between*. This wouldn't hamper his understanding an action seen on television, but he couldn't properly understand what is taking place when reading in a book, *The rabbit ran between the turnips.*

To teach these important words of relationship, you will need some small structure – a toy house or garage – that would permit you to move

Concept	%	Concept	%
Into	92	Hard	62
Open	89	Soft	61
Out of	89	Through	61
On top of	87	Many (apples)	60
Dirty	85	White	55
Under (a bridge or car)	84	Forward	55
Wet	84	Not move	55
Up	83	Light	54
Down	82	Biggest	53
Little	75	Rough	53
Big	75	Long	53
Moved	75	Short	53
Closed	73	Top	52
Empty	71	Dry	52
Clean	71	Smooth	50
One (apple)	70	Over	48
Under (furniture)	69	Far away	46
Full	69	Around	43
Next to	67	Bottom	38
Black	66	Side	35
Littlest	65	Backward	34
More	63		

Dr. Palmer's List of Concepts

some toy or animal around in relation to it. Or just cut a front and back 'door' in an empty facial tissue box to serve as a castle. Set a cup or some other object a few inches away. By positioning small toy figures around the castle, you can explain the meaning of *on, over, next to, through, around, near, far from, up, against, inside, outside, under, behind, between* (the castle and the cup) and the parts of the structure: *top, bottom, front, side, rear.* You might drive a toy car through the castle to explain *forward, backwards,* and even *sideways.* But remember, words indicating position are easy to confuse, so don't teach Baldwin more than one a day, and review it regularly.

While driving or walking with Baldwin, play a game of identifying words of position or placement: "Look, Baldwin, that airplane is *over* the houses. Can you see anything else that is *over* the houses. The clouds? Right! Can you see anything that is *over* our head? A tree. What's going *under* the tree? We are. Right! Can you see anything else that is *under* something?"

Adjectives

Adjectives, you may recall, are describing words. They tell us the special qualities of objects; for example, a *controversial* statement, a *dazzling* extravaganza, and a *Brobdingnagian* blunder. But we'll start your child off with simpler adjectives, those you use every day. Adjectives are both abundant and valuable.

big-small	hot-cold	tall-short	easy-difficult
hard-soft	new-old	open-closed	high-low
thick-thin	strong-weak	heavy-light	clean-dirty
full-empty	sweet-sour	wet-dry	smooth-rough

Though these adjectives are presented in pairs, don't teach them in pairs. Teaching a child, close together in time, two bits of related information can invite confusion – which may explain why some people confuse *left* with *right* or *east* with *west*. They were taught these pairs together and their initial uncertainty grew to become a continuing puzzlement. If you are teaching *wet*, then compare it to *not wet* instead of *dry*. A week or so later, when the child is thoroughly familiar with the term *wet* and the condition the word stands for, you can then safely introduce the special word we have for the non-wet state.

How to begin? Suppose you start with *empty*. Choose a bowl similar to the one holding Baldwin's cereal. "Your bowl has food in it – right, Baldwin? But this bowl doesn't have food in it. It's *empty*." Show him one or two more items that are empty. An empty glass compared to his glassful of milk, or an empty cup compared with your cup of coffee.

Does Baldwin know the main colors yet? These, too, are adjectives. Cut swatches of different colors from magazines, glue them to a sheet of paper and print the appropriate name beside each. Teach just one color at a time and review it often. "This is yellow, Baldwin. Can you see anything in the kitchen that is yellow? Banana. Right!" Encourage him to use each new word himself a few times. The more associations or links he forms with the word – by hearing it, by seeing it in print, and by speaking it – the more easily will he remember it. "What's this color again? Yellow. Right! And what color is the banana? Yellow, yes of course."

An effective way to teach the names of colors is to give the youngster a swatch of material or paper of a particular color and have him locate items around the home bearing that color.

When Baldwin is acquainted with the list of adjectives, and feels confident in using them – which may take a month or two – begin introducing the idea of degree or extent such as *high, higher, highest; hot, hotter, hottest,* continuing in this way with all other adjectives in the list. (Some words such as *open* and *closed* don't lend themselves to expressing extent or degree except as *more open, slightly open, nearly open,* and so on.)

Adjectives denoting quantity are important too. Counting is dealt with in Chapter 11. Read that chapter before attempting to teach Baldwin to count. For the moment, he can be taught the idea of *one* and *two*. But don't teach merely the words one and two. Show him the difference between one spoon and two spoons, one fork and two forks, one cup and two cups, and so on.

Other simple concepts of quantity can be taught with pennies, marbles, or poker chips; concepts such as *some, many, all, none, most, more, less* (*less* if in quantity, *fewer* if in the number of items). "Here, I'll give you *some* marbles, Lucretia, and I'll take *some* myself. Now I'll put *one* marble here for teddy bear. I can't give him *some* marbles because he has no fingers to hold them – right? Here, I'll give you *more* marbles. Perhaps I'll take *more* for myself."

As each new word is introduced, add it to your list so she can immediately see its printed form. Explain briefly any irregularity in letter-sound relationship that occurs – as, for example, in *some, none, rough, through.* Make a brief note of any difficulty Lucretia experiences and mention it to the tutors. They can then give extra time to the problem.

Wall to Wall Pictures

When Lucretia is reading well and has a first-hand understanding of the world around her, you can employ the two-dimensional world of pictures to extend her vocabulary.

Clip photos from picture magazines and attach slips of paper to them bearing the names of various objects depicted (as has been done in Figure 15). Old *National Geographic* magazines are a good source of pictures for vocabulary enrichment. Each picture will usually permit you to introduce several new words. For example, a photo of a square-rigged schooner might permit you to teach the words *ship, sail, wave, horizon, deck,* and other nautical terms.

Figure 15: *Using photos for vocabulary building.*

But note: this exercise would be pointless if children had never seen an actual boat and were unaware of its function; otherwise, a child might think a square-rigger was a differently shaped apartment building.

Each picture, with its several word slips in place, might then be affixed to a wall for review after tooth brushing and before the reading of bedtime stories. In fact, the various walls around the home – in the kitchen or dining area, in the child's bedroom, the bathroom, the foyer – might be turned into 'pages' of an immense vocabulary book. The youngster would read each word slip, locate the object in the photo and, if appropriate, describe its purpose. Review of the pictures can take the form of a game, each wall of pictures being considered a different 'island' for the youngster to visit in search of a treasure. The treasure might be paper clips that had been attached to some of the word slips beforehand. The child could receive a small treat for discovering and bringing back the paper clips from his explorative journey around the home. For preschoolers, valentines from a large book of press-out cards have proved popular.

A hint of adventure might be added if Lucretia assumed the role of a doctor visiting the islands to take care of sick people and animals. Let her suggest how she would like the exercise to run. Such ideas may not be earthshaking (in your opinion), but they'll be *hers*, and for that reason, they will captivate her.

Pictures might also be fastened to card stock and propped up for review at mealtimes or glued in a large scrapbook to make a picture dictionary: a book you may ultimately wish to keep as a souvenir of a particularly interesting period in your child's development.

If your tutors are able to print neatly, you might simply supply them with old magazines, paper, glue, and a felt-tip pen, and let them select and mount pictures suitable for the exercise. Old picture magazines can be bought cheaply at a used-book store.

Pictures you select for vocabulary growth should show, whenever possible, the object's function and it size in relation to people. A child might think a canoe to be the size of an ocean liner unless someone was shown in or beside it. And a picture of a wheelbarrow would mean little to a child unless someone was seen using it.

Sentence Lists

A particularly effective way to teach new words is to compose sentences that employ those words. Type or print the sentences on sheets for the child to read aloud once or twice a day for a number of days. For example,

> When something *improves*, it gets better.
> *Daily* means every day.
> When something is *ordinary*, there is nothing special about it.
> The sides of the door are *parallel*.

As a child's vocabulary grows, less common words can be introduced to the activity. The early Batman series was unusual in that it featured an astonishingly rich vocabulary (to titillate adult viewers in the tradition of children's pantomime) while providing the routine hi-jinks for children. A few excerpted sentences will give you an idea of the procedure.

> *"Let's ponder the crook's motive,"* said Batman. *Ponder* means to think about something. The *motive* is the reason a person does something.

> Batman said of the Joker, *"His insane conceit may betray him."* When someone has an extremely high opinion of his or her own ability, appearance, or worth, we say that person is *conceited*.

The plots of TV movies you have watched with your child can provide an interesting way to expand his or her vocabulary. In one home, incidents in movie plots were used to introduce the following italicized words.

> Thorndyke *eluded* his *captors* by following the *bed of a stream*. This *foiled* the dogs that were *tracking* his *scent*.

100

Dr. Samuel A. Mudd *set* the broken leg of John Wilkes Booth, the man who *assassinated* Lincoln. He was *accused* of *complicity* in the *plot* to kill Lincoln, had to *stand trial*, and was *convicted*.

Scott's *adventure* provided a *series* of *unbearable hardships* for himself and his men.

One can't predict which words taught in this way will lodge in a child's mind. Words that youngsters find no use for are soon forgotten. (Quizzed four years later, children knew all the words in the preceding sentences except *complicity*.)

Create your own sentences describing actions in some movie your son, Sergey, has seen but using words he doesn't know. After you have explained the meanings of the various words, have him read the sentences aloud each day.

Voice-over Television

Television is an excellent source of words for vocabulary expansion. Best if the program being viewed has been tape-recorded. Consider the picture tube as you would the page of a picture book. Use gaps between narration – or a flick of the 'pause' button – to teach words relevant to the pictured action. "That's called a *floatplane*, Sergey, and those two long things underneath it are called *floats* or *pontoons*. That large sailboat it's flying over is called a *yacht*." Keep a pad and pen handy to jot down any new words for review at a later time.

Encourage the child to ask the meaning of unknown words he hears in conversations and on TV. But be careful that in explaining the meaning of one word you don't use other words he doesn't know. If there isn't time to fill his request immediately, make a note of the word and discuss it later.

Finding Suitable TV Programs

A wide range of programs suitable for children can be found during the daytime on your local PBS station or provincial TV station. If you aren't at home during the day, you might tape them.

Use of the Dictionary

The dictionary will eventually fill an important role in Sergey's education. How indexing works is described in Chapter 13. Our purpose here is merely to acquaint him with the basic role of a dictionary while using it for vocabulary growth in a simplified way.

An ideal dictionary for this purpose is one that contains 20,000-30,000 entries and perhaps 1000 good-quality photos and drawings. To begin, we will concern ourselves only with the illustrations.

Leaf through the section containing words that begin with the letter A. Mark an X beside any pictured item Sergey already knows by name. Also mark an X beside any pictured item that is beyond his present vocabulary needs; for example, the words *acropolis, acute angle,* and *apogee,* if illustrated, are of interest only to highly advanced youngsters. Such words, and those he already knows, will be left out of the exercise.

In the following exercise – one well suited to a tutor's management – Sergey merely reads aloud dictionary entries for those pictures that are *not* marked with an X. Four such entries might be read each day, with a review of earlier entries.

A simple game can be made of the procedure by placing one, two, three, four, five, or six dots beside the various pictures. The child then rolls a die to determine which of the various entries to read. Or, by marking pictures with symbols or colors, a different sort of die (obtainable at educational toy stores) might be used. This could provide an imaginative way to familiarize him with geometric shapes and their names.

You or your tutors should show Sergey how to use the pronunciation code and encourage him to learn how to use it. When he completes the entries in the A section of the dictionary, mark the illustrations in the B section and continue.

Enterprising Conversation

Your conversations with Sergey can be a highly effective means of increasing his vocabulary. When chatting, don't limit yourself to words he knows. Use words he *doesn't* know then explain their meaning. For example, if he expresses awe at a high-priced car, instead of saying, "It costs a lot of money," say "It's an expensive car, Sergey. *Expensive* means it costs more than most other cars. Look, there's another *expensive* car over there. Can you say *expensive*? Good, what kind of car is it again?" Find occasion to use any new word two or three times and encourage him to use the word himself.

Visits to museums and other centers of learning provide an engaging way to enlarge a child's vocabulary. And the program of 'educational opportunism', which will be described later, provides a natural, never-ending source of words.

An Early Rich Vocabulary

John Burdon Sanderson Haldane, geneticist, biometrician, physiologist and popularizer of science and the philosophy of biology was always up to mischief as a boy. When the youngster injured his forehead at age five, he studied the blood and asked, "Is it oxyhaemoglobin or carboxyhaemoglobin?"

10

Spelling, Printing, and Writing

The activities described in this chapter are primarily for children who can read; though even non-readers will benefit from some of the activities.

We have now reached a limit in what can be achieved by a program of convenience education. Spelling can be pursued at mealtimes and while shopping, but printing and writing will have to be handled by tutors or by parents willing to give extra time to teaching. You will best decide whether you wish to pursue these activities, and if so, how. I will proceed as if you intended to engage your child in these activities without help.

Spelling, printing and writing exercises are not as entertaining for children as reading. But children's interest can be sustained if parents keep the activities brief and fun-filled. So, while you proceed with spelling, printing and writing, you might also incorporate material from Chapter 11, *Counting, Measuring, and Computing*. Then, there is your continuing pursuit of vocabulary enrichment, and finally, for diversion, there are the mazes, the visual acuity puzzles and the memory game in Chapter 12.

Spelling

'Inventive spelling' is now entrenched in some public school classrooms. Pupils are invited to spell words in any way they wish. Their invented or imagined spelling is accepted as correct. In short, it's goodbye English language as we know it. But wait. There are still plenty of people who prefer traditional spelling, so it might be a while before we are back to scratching pictures on cave walls.

Children are sometimes taught to spell at the same time they are being taught to read – a mistake that has created needless confusion in their minds between letter-sounds and letter-names. Children have no need to know the names of letters – *ay, bee, see, dee,* and the others – until they begin learning to spell. If your child is now able to read skillfully, he or she can safely proceed with spelling.

Skip the vowels for the moment; begin with the letter **B**. Tell Omar that **B**, and its lower-case form, **b**, is called *bee.* Have him pick out and name upper- and lower-case **B**s in newspapers or magazine text.

Next, teach him the name for **C** (*see*). Ask him to pick out and name some upper- and lower-case **C**s and **B**s. Continue in this way through the alphabet – **D** (dee), **F** (eff) and so on, leaving **A**, **E**, **I**, **O**, and **U**, until the last.

To give Omar practice in distinguishing between letter-sounds and letter-names, play 'I Spy' while eating, driving or shopping – a game you perhaps already know. To begin, announce, "I spy with my little eye something that begins with ..." then supply the *name* of a letter, not its phonic sound. Omar must then look around to find items beginning with the appropriate letter. He probably won't show much skill at first, so tell him the answer. Now it's his turn. Of course, he'll give away the answer by looking at the object before he poses the problem. What do you do? You provide a few wrong answers to delight him, or have the puppet whisper some outrageous answers in your ear. Omar will soon be laughing merrily as he learns.

When, after some time, Omar has learned the *names* of the letters and can name each one in a line of print – whether in capital letters or lower-case letters – he will be able to play spelling games.

Spelling Games

You can play spelling games while eating, driving, shopping or walking. Begin with simple words: "Do you know how to spell *dog*, Magnolia?" She probably won't be able to, so spell it for her, voicing first, the three letter-sounds then the names of each letter – roughly, *duh, aw, guh,* then *dee, oh, jee.* This practice will show her that the way to correctly spell a word can sometimes be learned by first sounding the individual components of a word.

Having sounded and named the letters in *dog*, it's her turn: "I'll bet you can spell it now." Let her spell it, helping if necessary. A minute later, ask her to spell *dog* again. Repetition is the key to speedy progress. A useful tack is to say, "You've probably forgotten how to spell *dog*, haven't you?" then explode with surprise and delight when she spells it. Have her spell *dog* for you a few more times, expressing astonishment each time she remembers how to do so. And later, make a production of her accomplishment for your spouse: "Magnolia can spell *dog* now, dear. Isn't that wonderful? No, I'm not kidding. OK, Magnolia, let Daddy hear it."

Over a period of weeks, advance gradually from short, simple words – *car, cat, sky, road* – to longer words: *bicycle, crane, bridge, avenue, people, building.* If, by learning a few spelling rules, children were enabled to spell *all* words correctly, poor spellers would be unknown. Unfortunately, this isn't the case. Words are sometimes inconsistent in their spelling, hence *bicycle* and *icicle, glue* and *flu.* Repetition alone will equip Magnolia with that rare and enviable ability to spell correctly. She may need to be reminded several times before she can master the trickier words.

Magnolia will particularly enjoy the Sign Game because she can hardly make a mistake and, as you know, children like to appear clever. While in the car waiting for the light to change, look at a sign (making sure Magnolia sees where you are looking) and select a word – perhaps the word *new*, and say, "Magnolia, do you know how to spell *new*?" Of course she does! She can spell the word just by naming the letters on the sign. Mild astonishment on your part, and plenty of praise, will fire her interest in the game. When the sign is lost from view, immediately ask her again if she can spell *new* and congratulate her again for getting it right. Continue this procedure every few minutes, gradually lengthening the time you request to half an hour. Will she become bored? Not if your astonishment makes her giggle and burst with pride.

The Sign Game can be altered slightly for play at mealtimes using various food labels and packaging. For example, point to the word *cereal* on the breakfast food carton and ask her if she can spell it. When she has named the letters, turn the carton so she can't see the word and ask her if she can still spell *cereal.* Your delight will fuel her interest in the game. A minute later, ask her again. Five minutes later repeat your request, then again after a ten-minute interval. If you quiz her at gradually lengthening intervals, she will still remember how to spell the word at bedtime and the following morning.

For variation, while eating, spell aloud the name of some item within view: *fork, cup, spoon, bowl,* and print it on a piece of paper for Magnolia to see. Ask her to spell the item while she can see your list. Turn the list face down and see if she can still spell the word. Gradually lengthen the time before asking her to spell the word again. Continue on, similarly, one at a time with the other words.

Soon, Magnolia will realize that her knowledge of the letter sounds helps her to spell many words; that, for example, by speaking the word *caramel* slowly, its sound conveys clues to the sequence of letters that need be strung together to form that sound. As her ability to spell advances, she will begin to pay closer attention to the spelling of words she sees around her and in books. Having gained elementary skill in spelling, Magnolia is equipped to begin printing. But first she must learn to control a writing tool.

Controlling a Pencil

Learning to hold and manipulate a pencil may take several months of practice. Show your youngster, Imran, how to hold a pencil. A pencil having a triangular shape will help him position his thumb and fingers correctly. When he is scribbling or coloring (even with crayons) encourage him to hold the instrument in a way that is suitable for writing. Solving mazes (page 129) promotes careful guidance with a pencil, and the diligent spotter activity (page 143) also requires careful marking.

The following activities will provide additional practice in manipulating a pencil. Tell Imran you are going to show him how to make print pictures. Place tracing paper (or onion skin paper, obtainable at a stationer's) over a word in a newspaper headline and show Imran how you can trace around the letters with a pencil or pen. When he sees how words can be 'lifted' from the page in this way, he'll be eager to do the same. Tape the tracing paper so it stays in position until he finishes his 'print picture'.

In large letters, print words that Imran finds fascinating; chief among them being his name. Imran's maturity will determine what other words he would like to trace; perhaps *bomb, jet, doctor*. If you are unsure of your ability to print neatly, type his words in some slender typeface. If you don't have a computer and printer, perhaps you have access to someone else's. Type the word or words, highlight them, insert whatever point-size you want (75, 100, 125 or more) in the point-size window and click Enter. Imran will then have large letters to trace.

Treat Imran's tracings as works of art. Post them prominently on a wall or door. Invite friends and neighbors to view the exhibition (making sure, of course, that Imran is present to note their attention and admiration).

Imran might be encouraged to trace cartoon characters from comic strips. It matters little whether he traces letters or comics; both exercises will develop his skill in manipulating a pencil.

Carbon paper can provide yet another fascinating activity. Show Imran how carbon paper works and show him how to trace figures or designs from publications onto paper. If you attach a piece of paper with masking tape behind the figure Imran intends to copy, leaving three sides unattached so the carbon paper can be inserted, Imran will be able to lift the top page occasionally to see how his copy is progressing, and do so without losing registration.

A department store mail-order catalog or almost any advertising matter delivered to your home will provide another engaging exercise. With a pen or pencil, Imran can add beards, moustaches and spectacles to the various faces of models in the advertisements. Perhaps hats and jewelry can be added to the figures, and patterns added to any plain clothing.

Figure 16: *Drawing funny faces encourages children to use a pencil.*

Give Imran blank paper and show him how to draw funny faces. Those shown in Figure 16 are easy to draw. If paper is scarce in your home, use the backs of flyers that arrive at the door or in the mail. Or, you might purchase a type of drawing pad on which the drawing can be repeatedly erased by lifting the front plastic sheet away from the black waxed backing, available in most toy stores.

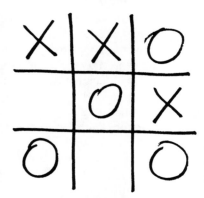

Figure 17: *A completed game of Ticktacktoe showing a win for the Os.*

A spirograph entices the manipulation of a pencil, as do plastic stencils. Still another way to encourage use of a pencil is to play ticktacktoe with Imran. When playing the game, let Imran draw the grids, thus providing added exercise with the pencil. Be sure Imran always wins the game and he'll be eager to play five or six games with you during supper and perhaps five or six more later with the tutor. If Imran begins to suspect you are deliberately letting him win, have him play against the puppet (described on page 69). The puppet, being a dull fellow will, of course, make all sorts of blunders in playing the game – to Imran's amusement.

Lists, Lists, Lists

Once your daughter, Gretel, has a basic knowledge of printing, she needs plenty of practice to advance in both printing and in spelling. An exercise that advances both these abilities in an enjoyable manner is the printing of lists. Show Gretel how she can create lists of things she likes, helping her when necessary with the spelling. Here are a few suggested lists that interest most youngsters.

> Some ways I like to travel
> Flowers I like
> Wild animals I like
> Tame animals I like
> Toys I like
> Things I like to do
> Things I like to eat
> Things I would like to see
> Birds I have seen

Perhaps there are other lists Gretel would like to create. As each list (containing six or more items) is finished, post it conspicuously. Purchase some colorful peel-off animal stickers at the stationers and attach one to each list as a seal of approval.

Another valuable exercise is to have Gretel print your shopping lists for you, again, helping her with the spelling. And when you go shopping, see that Gretel is equipped with a pad and pencil to print the names of items that interest her. Her printed lists of items at the supermarket will be sure to win compliments from Daddy, Aunt Cynthia, Grandma, and others.

On another occasion, you might appeal to Gretel's generosity, and help her compose a list for Daddy, or some other relative, called *Things I would like to buy for you*. What a hit the list will be with the recipient!

Encourage Gretel to make a list of the books she reads: a job she can handle without help simply by copying the spelling from the cover of each book. Post the list prominently so she can add new titles as she finishes each book.

Just a Reminder

Explain to Gretel that a memorandum, or memo, is a note we make for ourselves so we won't forget to do something. Encourage her to make memos for tasks to be done on the morrow: WATER THE DANDELIONS, FEED THE GOLDFISH, GET A BAG OF FOOD FOR SCAMP, and so on. By leaving these brief notes for herself in a place where she will be sure to see them the next day, Gretel will develop a sense of system and responsibility.

> ### The Value of Reminders
>
> The eminent all-round man of science, J.B.S. Haldane could read by his third birthday. By the age of five he had been taught German by his nurse, and could write well enough to leave small notes scattered about the house inscribed, *"I hate you."*

To increase the volume of Gretel's printing, reward her for printing in a way that invites still more printing. Children love to print the names of items on self-adhering labels and attach the labels to the appropriate objects: *door, wall, chair, table,* and so on. To illustrate, Gretel might be asked to find four words in her dictionary that interest her. She could print the four words in a lined exercise book, called Gretel's Dictionary Book. For entering the four words in her book, Gretel might receive four blank self-adhering labels. She would then print the names of any four items around the home (receiving help with the spelling), and attach the labels to those items. The four words Gretel printed in her Dictionary Book could be discussed at suppertime, thereby reinforcing whatever understanding she has already formed of the words.

Perhaps you occasionally send letters by mail instead of by e-mail. Could Gretel print a brief message for inclusion? She might also send letters to Santa Claus at the appropriate time, and letters to the Tooth Fairy – in preparation for teeth that will eventually be falling out or just as a sort of dental report. Are there sales people you repeatedly encounter while shopping? If Gretel printed a brief note to give to that person – *Hello, I like you. Gretel* – receipt of her message would brighten the recipient's day.

Encourage Gretel to print and post signs, perhaps beginning with one for the door of her bedroom: GRETEL'S ROOM, WELCOME, PLEASE KNOCK, THANK YOU. Would you like some signs for your own bedroom? She might also print and post signs for the kitchen: BEWARE OF STOVE, KNIVES ARE DANGEROUS. How about some general signs concerning safety, cleanliness, or tidiness: DON'T LITTER, WIPE YOUR FEET, PLEASE, and possibly one for the supper table: WASH YOUR HANDS, PLEASE.

When Gretel has learned to master basic control of a writing tool, she can hone this skill by means of an ingenious system that advances either printing or writing. Educational Fontware, Inc (www.educationalfontsware.com) offers various computer programs that let you create text made up of dots. By tracing around the dots, a child learns to print or write correctly and neatly. This system is used at the Institute to create stories for the children to trace in both printed and written form. Each episode of the story ends mysteriously, thus assuring children's continued interest. And to increase their interest even more, a child's own name appears in each section of story. The following example illustrates the procedure and serves to show how you might employ this engaging exercise.

> **Episode 1:** *One day, Gretel saw a large black ball. As she watched the ball it made an eerie sound and suddenly became smaller.*

> **Episode 2:** *To her surprise, the ball slowly ascended to the ceiling, and Gretel heard a strange laugh.*

> **Episode 3:** *As Gretel watched, a light appeared inside the ball and it began rolling back and forth across the ceiling.*

> **Episode 4:** *The ball plummeted to the floor and broke. What do you suppose Gretel saw? A dwarf with hairy ears and three eyes.*

And so on. When you create a story of this sort, employ a few words that Gretel doesn't know and explain their meaning to her in advance. The exercise then becomes a means of enlarging her vocabulary.

There might be other words or names she might like to trace. Create them as dotted words for printing or, if she has advanced to writing, in written form.

The Great Encyclopedia Quiz Game

This advanced activity is suitable for children who are now reading and printing (or writing) and have learned quantities (dealt with in Chapter 11). The special delight of the encyclopedia quiz game is that it makes youngsters appear to be clever. Give Sean a lined exercise book, perhaps imprinted with an impressive title: *The Encyclopedia Quiz-Kid's Book*. Next, show him how to compose interesting questions from encyclopedia entries. For example, leafing through the encyclopedia, he might chance upon the entry for the ostrich. On reading about ostriches, he would learn these immense birds lay eggs that are six inches (or fifteen centimeters) long, and weigh three pounds (or more than one kilogram).

Show Sean how to compose sentences in his quiz book.

> How long is an ostrich egg? *Six inches.*

> How heavy is an ostrich egg? *Three pounds.*

Then, flipping through another volume, he might find an entry for elephants. On reading the text, he could compose two more interesting questions.

> How many kinds of elephants are there? *Two, the African and Indian elephants.*

> Do female elephants have tusks? *Only the African elephants.*

When Sean sees he has the means of teaching you and your spouse, he'll be delighted to compose questions each day for suppertime quizzing.

Another obvious benefit from the encyclopedia quiz is that it leads children to self-education; this, being the most important, yet most overlooked, component of any educational system.

Paying Bills

The well-educated six- or seven-year-old, now able to write, will be able to pay the monthly bills for you – at least, those bills you don't pay by telephone, on-line, or by automatic withdrawal. The exercise introduces Sean to elementary business practice. The following notice, affixed to the wall, will provide adequate guidance for paying bills and expanding his vocabulary.

Invoice Processing Procedure

1. Make out a check for the correct amount as per specimen. (Affix a check for, say, the telephone company, for a stated amount, dated, and signed.)
2. Address an envelope if an envelope doesn't accompany the bill.
3. Stick a stamp on the envelope.
4. Record the letter in the Mailing Book.
5. Present check for my signature, along with the envelope.

And Now, an Important Message

If Sean is old enough to observe socially acceptable conduct, yet seems to need constant reminding, his oversights can be used to advance his penmanship. The educational value of writing 'lines' – a practice as old as teaching – can play a valuable part in your program. If asked to write a memorandum to himself ten or more times, Sean might – just might – stop an offensive practice. The following examples might strike a familiar chord in your memory.

> *I must not leave a wet towel on the bathroom floor.*
> *I must remember to flush the toilet.*
> *I shouldn't leave my clothes lying on the bedroom floor.*

You might think of other social lapses that could benefit from written reminders.

Letter writing is not the art it once was; the telephone and E-mail have reduced the need for penned letters. Still, children like to send brief notes to others living in remote areas of the world. To find a pen pal for Sean you could contact the board of education in some city via your internet search engine. A list of elementary schools and their addresses may be listed there; otherwise, e-mail a note to the board itself similar to the following.

> *My (four- five- or six-year-old) son, Sean, would like to correspond with someone at one of your schools. Though he is young, Sean is quite advanced. I hope you might be able to pass on this request to a suitable youngster or parent.*

You may find that Sean derives far greater pleasure from receiving letters than from writing them, and is usually at a loss for thinking of matters to mention. Solution? Each time he discusses something with you – something he has just seen or heard – have him write it down to compose a list of topics he can describe in his next letter.

11

Counting and Measuring

The fact that there are 40,000 muscles in an elephant's trunk or that the world's smallest mammal (the fat-tailed shrew) is just an inch-and-a-half long would not astonish a child who didn't know how much 40,000 was or how long an inch was. Let's consider, therefore, those quantities and measurements that permit children to better understand the world around them.

Counting

Some primitive peoples have only three numbers or categories in their counting: *one, two*, and *many*. The idea has apparently never occurred to them that single increases above two, if given names equivalent to our *three, four, five,* when memorized, would let them carry around in their heads a 'ruler made of words': a ruler with which they could measure, and record various quantities. The word-ruler that you and I carry around in our head has virtually no limit to its reaches except, of course, for the length of time needed to count as high as we wish.

When we teach children to count, we begin with the first short length of the word ruler, from one to ten. However, when children recite *One, two, three, four, five, six, seven, eight, nine, ten,* the sounds they voice have no more meaning than *Mary had a little lamb*. A recitation of sounds doesn't convey any relationship between its component sounds and visible increments of quantity (which is why the sounds *one* and *two* were taught earlier in combination with objects: *one spoon, two spoons,* and so on),

Let's assume that Marcus has learned to count two objects. *one spoon, two spoons.* We can now extend his ability to *three spoons.* But don't push ahead too quickly with *four, five* and *six.* Remember these are new words to him, and vocabulary growth is a slow business. Wait until Marcus has used the new word *three* several times in counting objects – *three plates, three pots, three jars,* and so on – before advancing to the word *four.*

By teaching just one new counting word every day or two, Marcus will be counting to one hundred in about half that number of days. While learning to count to one hundred, Marcus should count only objects he sees, rather than recite numbers. When he has learned to count to ten, you might find yourself running short of spoons for him to count, so change to marbles or pennies. And now, Marcus can stop naming the item he is counting. That is to say, instead of counting "One penny, two pennies, three pennies," he need only count "One, two, three." When the child reaches twenty, you may want to begin counting some items you have in greater supply: pieces of uncooked macaroni, dried beans, or similar commodities.

On reaching thirty, Marcus will easily be able count from thirty to thirty-nine when he sees the progression is similar to that used in counting through the twenties. But don't rush ahead with *forty* until two or three days have passed and *twenty* and *thirty* are clear in his mind. Continue slowly in this way gradually introducing the new words *forty, fifty, sixty,* and so on up to one hundred.

When Marcus reaches one hundred he will need more practice in order to count quickly and correctly to one hundred. This can provide a game while you are driving or walking. For example, one player voices the odd numbers while the other fills in with the even numbers. Counting the even numbers is more difficult for children because they must introduce each new tens group: twenty, thirty, forty. So, let Marcus count the odd numbers. When he eventually gains skill and confidence, then he can count the even numbers. To add variety, each player might count two or three numbers in succession. While you are driving, look for items to count: mailboxes, fire hydrants, trucks, or anything else that is plentiful.

To encourage counting – which, admittedly, can become tedious – you might provide an incentive to sustain Marcus's interest. Four- and five-year-olds in one home received a card from a large book of press-out valentines every time they counted to 100. In a week they had reduced the book to a skeleton of borders and their counting was quick and accurate.

When Marcus can count to 100, encourage him to count to 1,000. Progressing a little higher each day, this task could take him a week or two. Have him begin counting where he left off the previous day. On reaching 1,000, Marcus will be a skillful counter. And yet, he will have only a rough idea of what this quantity means. He should see a thousand objects to understand how immense that number is.

To show him what a large quantity of objects looks like, we need a suitable vehicle. Rice serves our purpose well. Take a heaping teaspoon of rice. Tip it onto a plate and count how many you have. The number will vary with the type of rice you use. I found there to be roughly 200 in one heaping teaspoon of unhusked rice.

"Let's suppose, Marcus, that we're up in a helicopter in the Arctic Circle and we're looking down on a herd of reindeer. Each grain of rice here is reindeer. Let's see what a herd of 200 would look like." Pour out one heaping teaspoonful of rice. "That's quite a few, isn't it? Let's look at 400." Pour out another heaping teaspoon of rice. By successively adding teaspoons, you can show Marcus 600, 800, and 1,000.

"Some people living far in the north have 10,000 or 12,000 reindeer in their herds. Let's see what a herd that large would look like." One heaping tablespoon holds about four heaping teaspoonfuls – that's 800 grains of rice. Seven-and-a-half heaping tablespoonfuls fill a measuring cup (about 220 milliliters) – that's 6000 grains. A little arithmetic tells us that 367 ml of rice would give us 10,000 grains and 440 ml would give us 12,000.

For Marcus to understand one million would require 167 cupfuls of rice. Not many homes keep this quantity on hand. Instead, buy sheets of metric graph paper that have been squared in millimeters. Glue several such sheets edge to edge to form a large square one-meter by one-meter. This would contain a million tiny squares. Stick the square meter to your wall. This could be interesting for adults too. Not many have ever seen an exact million of anything.

Distance

To teach Juanita short distances, produce a ruler and show her what an inch or a centimeter is. Explain that rulers help us to understand things. For example, when Uncle Sam tells us over the phone that he caught a fish eleven inches (or twenty-eight centimeters) long, we can look at our ruler and see how big the fish was.

Juanita will enjoy measuring items on the supper table. Make a list of the objects she measures, marking down the measurements she gives you. For the moment, ignore fractions. Show her how to measure to the nearest inch or centimeter. If she doesn't know the meaning of *height, width, length,* and *thickness,* this is a good time to teach her those terms. Have her measure the height of a ketchup bottle, the length of a spoon, the distance across a cup (no need to mention *diameter* at this moment), and the dimensions of other items at hand.

Eventually, Juanita will be able to play a game of estimating distances. To play, she is to ask you how long or how tall various objects are, then measure them to see how close your estimate was.

When Juanita gains skill in measuring small objects, give her a yardstick (or meter stick) and explain its relationship to the short ruler she was using. You might mention that detectives observe distances and dimensions very closely, and they have to be certain about the size of various objects. Then send her off with a pad, pencil, and yardstick to measure anything she pleases around the home. Or, you could suggest projects for her. You might ask her to see if she can find the length and width of the kitchen table, the height of the chairs, the size of her bed and any other objects she chooses. High on her list of preferences, of course, would be how tall she is. And how tall are you?

To teach Juanita how far a mile is, or a kilometer, refer to the odometer in your car while driving. Note some landmark situated a mile, or a kilometer, from your home. Constant reminders of this distance while traveling to or from your home will familiarize her with this distance. You might then note landmarks that are two, three, or four miles or kilometers from your home.

Another way to familiarize Juanita with the distance conveyed by a mile is to walk that distance with her. A city map will let you find an intersection of streets that are situated a mile or kilometer from your home. Perhaps Juanita could count the number of steps she takes to reach that spot.

Weight

Estimating weight is an entertaining activity at fairs. It can provide entertainment at mealtimes too. Begin by teaching your son, Alnur, how much an ounce or a gram is. Kitchen scales are usually too insensitive to measure small weights so you might buy an inexpensive letter scale for this purpose.

Make a chart on which Alnur can keep track of everything he measures. How much does a pen weight? A spoon? The saltshaker? Scissors? When he has gained a basic understanding of measuring weight, bring an assortment of objects to the supper table and play a weighing game with him. He hands you some item. You estimate its weight and mark your estimate on a piece of paper. Alnur weighs the object and tells you how wrong you were. Or perhaps he congratulates you.

Depending on how measurements are recorded in your part of the world, teach Alnur there are sixteen ounces in a pound, or 1000 grams in a kilogram, then continue the game with heavier objects, using the kitchen scale to verify their weights. For even heavier items, use your bathroom scale. If an object won't fit on the scale, stand on the scale holding the item, then subtract your weight from the total. How much does a kitchen chair weigh? A tricycle? The cat? The dog?

118

Finally, Alnur should be taught to understand the meaning of a ton, or tonne in metric. Explain that small cars weigh about a ton, that rhinoceroses weigh two or three tons, and that a large elephant might weigh five tons.

Liquid Measurement

Teach young Camilla that there are two pints in a quart and four quarts in a gallon – or that there are 1000 milliliters in a liter – depending on the measuring container you have handy. How much liquid goes into Camilla's cup or mug? Don't forget, you are not only teaching her volumes, you are also teaching her new words to describe those volumes, and vocabulary growth must proceed slowly.

When you are at a service station, let Camilla see a 50-gallon drum (used in many garages as garbage containers). How many cups of milk would a 50-gallon drum hold? *Not* a zillion.

Computing

There is more to counting than meets the eye. There are, in fact, four elements or components to the task. First, Camilla must learn the vocal utterances that stand for increases in quantity: the sounds represented in print by *one, two, three,* and so on. These sounds must then be matched with items to let her to see the relationship between sounds and objects: *one spoon, two spoons, three spoons.* Next, the child must learn to read the printed sequences of letters – one, two, three, four, five, six – that we use to indicate vocal increments. And finally, she must learn that that the ciphers 1, 2, 3 can substitute for both the utterances and for the printed words. A complex business, isn't it?

We will deal only with simple day-to-day calculating needs: adding, subtracting, multiplying, and dividing. Lionel's first need is to learn the shorthand – the ciphers 1, 2, 3 – we use to speed our computing. Explain to him that instead of writing words for numbers, we use signs for them – a sort of code. Show Lionel that in our mathematical code, *one* appears as 1, *two* appears as 2. The numbers on the next page will help him sort out and remember the signs we use to represent the numbers from *one* to *nine.*

Each cipher has the word for that cipher printed beneath it and each contains the number of circles the number represents. Lionel can always count the circles or read the word if he wants to assure himself that everything is correct. Photocopy page 120, place tracing paper over the copy and secure the paper so it won't slip under his rough handling.

Figure 18: *The numerical code.*

Lionel will then be able to trace each number, drawing through the middle of each circle.

When he can remember the various symbols and the quantities they stand for, he is ready to begin adding.

Adding

Set this book, open at page 120, on a bookstand so Leanne can refer to the numbers whenever she wishes. Explain that there are two other symbols in our code. The first is +, which means *plus* or *and.* The second, =, which means *is the same as.*

Bring a few dried beans or pieces of macaroni to the table. Place one bean in front of her. "If I add another bean to that one, Leanne, how many would there be?" She will know from counting spoons that there are now two. Let her see how this state of affairs would be shown in our code: $1 + 1 = 2$. Show her how the coded statement agrees with the number of dots shown on the numbers in Figure 18 and that the dots on each side of *is the same as* 'sign' are true. Show her that the coded statement is still true when reversed: $2 = 1 + 1$.

"All right, we have two beans. What if I add another bean. How many would there be now?" Add the bean. Leanne will see that there are now three. Once again, show her how this situation would be expressed $(2 + 1 = 3)$ and show her that this coded statement is consistent with the dots on the special numbers. Finally, change the order of numbers and let her see that $1 + 2 = 3$ and also that $3 = 1 + 2$.

This procedure will seem very simple to you, but it isn't simple for Leanne. You have shifted aside a curtain on a whole new world. She must get a mental purchase on the new information in her own way and in her own good time. When, after a few days or weeks, this information has dropped into place in Leanne's frame of logic, advance again slowly.

Now you might take a different approach. Place four beans on the table and mark down $= 4$. Give Leanne four beans and ask her to how the beans might be separated. If she separates them in two groups of two, mark her grouping $2 + 2 = 4$ and show her that this is consistent with the dots on the special numbers. If she divides her four beans into groups of one and three, mark that grouping, $1 + 3 = 4$.

Continue in this way from day to day using more beans and new numbers. You may find that what she learns one day may be forgotten the next. Children are not aware that the information $1 + 1 = 2$ or $1 + 2 = 3$ is something to be remembered for future use; therefore, an important part of her daily exercise should consist of repeating the sums she has already dealt with. When Leanne has progressed up to number

6, for example, her daily adding – possibly under the tutor's guidance – would be:

$1 + 1 =$ $1 + 2 =$ $2 + 1 =$ $3 + 1 =$ $1 + 3 =$

$2 + 2 =$ $1 + 4 =$ $4 + 1 =$ $2 + 3 =$ $3 + 2 =$

$1 + 5 =$ $5 + 1 =$ $2 + 4 =$ $4 + 2 =$ $3 + 3 =$

When Leanne can add 5 + 4 and 4 + 5, show her a shorter way that sums can be presented – with numbers placed one above the other. Continue to show the plus sign in each case so she won't be confused when she deals with subtraction and multiplication. Here are the problems Leanne will now have covered, shown in the new form. She may need help working with these until she becomes accustomed to the new presentation.

1	1	2	1	3	2	3	2	4	1	1
+1	+2	+1	+3	+1	+2	+2	+3	+1	+4	+5

5	2	4	3	6	1	2	5	4	3	1
+1	+4	+2	+3	+1	+6	+5	+2	+3	+4	+7

7	2	6	5	3	4	8	1	2	7	5
+1	+6	+2	+3	+5	+4	+1	+8	+7	+2	+4

4	3	6
+5	+6	+3

Writing out this many sums for Leanne each day could become burdensome. You might therefore have photocopies made and let her fill in a new sheet each day. Or affix a sheet of tracing paper over the sums. Her answers would then be marked on the tracing paper.

You may find Leanne counting on her fingers to aid adding. Or she might make dots beside each number and count the dots. Don't discourage either of these practices. Children drop these aids voluntarily when they gain skill and confidence in adding.

There are different theories about what children should be told when they encounter the number ten – 10 – one belief being they should be told that the 1 is in the tens column, and there is nothing in the units column. This information is perfectly true, but like the workings of an automobile transmission, it can be confusing for a child. Better to just say that 1 and 0 stands for ten, and drop the matter.

Mental adding can now become a pastime while driving or walking, but keep the sums easy until she gains confidence. "How much is one tree and one tree, Leanne?" Let her quiz *you* occasionally – which is still good practice for her because she will have to verify the accuracy of your answers. What if you give her a wrong answer? Try it and see. The puppet could play a role in this.

If you continue to enlarge the size of the sums and give Leanne daily practice in adding, she will soon be adding skillfully: an ability that, despite the availability of pocket calculators, continues to be of value.

Extracurricular Math

Many years ago, an innovative high-school teacher of my acquaintance gave after-school detentions that were either long or short depending on one's ability to add quickly and correctly. He would chalk up an immense addition on the blackboard (green chalkboards were unknown then, and so were pocket calculators) eight or nine figures wide and twelve or more figures high. As each offender (his detention periods always had good turnouts) arrived at the correct answer, he was free to leave.

Needless to say, pupils who constantly created problems in class became regular attendants at his detention periods – and they became exceptionally swift and precise at adding. Of the ways that children might be punished for misdemeanors in the home, adding is possibly the least damaging to a parent-child relationship. Regrettably, the effectiveness of adding as a punitive exercise gradually diminishes. Children become so skilful at adding they begin to take pride in their uncommon ability and almost welcome each opportunity to demonstrate their skill.

Subtraction

Subtraction is merely the reverse of adding. Follow the same simple steps you did with adding, but in reverse. Show Flavius the symbol for subtraction (–) and explain to him that this means *take away*. "Here are two beans, Flavius. Now, if I take one bean away, how many would be left? One. Right!" Show him this transaction in coded form: $2 - 1 = 1$. Continue in this way, progressing gradually to more beans and larger numbers, and make subtraction a game in the car.

You will eventually have to explain 'borrowing' from the left-hand column. Show Flavius how, in the problem below, the 7 is reduced to a 6, and the 3 becomes 13.

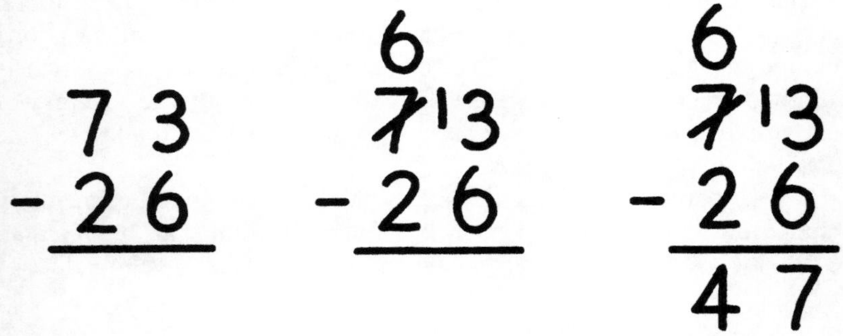

$$
\begin{array}{r} 7\ 3 \\ -2\ 6 \\ \hline \end{array}
\qquad
\begin{array}{r} 6 \\ \not{7}\ ^1 3 \\ -2\ 6 \\ \hline \end{array}
\qquad
\begin{array}{r} 6 \\ \not{7}\ ^1 3 \\ -2\ 6 \\ \hline 4\ 7 \end{array}
$$

Figure 19: *'Borrowing' in subtraction.*

Multiplication

Multiplication can be taught in a simple way. "Look, Flavius, suppose we went to the supermarket and bought a loaf of bread. Then, when we got home, we decided that one loaf wasn't enough, so we went back and bought another loaf. How many loaves would we have now? Two? Correct." Show Flavius how these purchases might be written down (example A in Figure 20); which, unfortunately, has the same form as an adding problem. Introduce the multiplication sign (x) to him.

A

1 loaf
X 2 trips
2 loaves

B

2 cans of soup
X 2 trips
4 cans of soup

Figure 20: *Multiplication can be taught by imagining trips to the store.*

"Now, suppose we made a trip to the store, Flavius, and bought two cans of soup, then I decided we needed two more; so, we went back again and bought two more cans. How many cans of soup would we have?" (Show him as has been done at B in Figure 20.) Continue in his way, proposing each time two trips for the imaginary purchase of three apples, four grapefruit, five lemons, six bananas, and so on up to ten items.

Don't forget the important contribution a puppet can make to your instruction by offering ridiculous answers or demanding absurd food items such as rubber-band sandwiches, chocolate-covered Ping-Pong balls, Kentucky-fried dew worms and so on.

Teach the three-times table by engaging in three imaginary trips to the store. Flavius may see that multiplication is similar to adding, and that three times two is really two plus two plus two.

Show Flavius that the purchases made on the various shopping trips can be entered on a chart, as has been done as A of Fig. 21 (next page). Make an enlarged photocopy of the blank grid shown at B and as Flavius gains skill with the two- and three-times tables, let him place a piece of tracing paper over the blank grid and fill in the answers he now knows.

Division

Fortunately, problems in division don't look like problems in adding, subtracting or multiplying. Place four beans on the table and ask Flavius to make two groups of the beans with the same number of beans in the two groups. You might have to help him. Then show him how this separation is described in coded form (A in Fig. 22), and how the answer would appear.

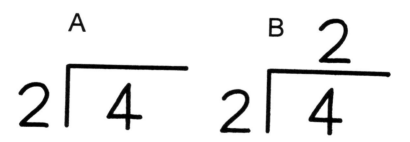

Figure 22: *A division problem, and its solution.*

Now ask Flavius to divide six beans into two equal groups. When he has done so, show him how the problem would be written down and what the answer would be. You might draw his attention to the fact that

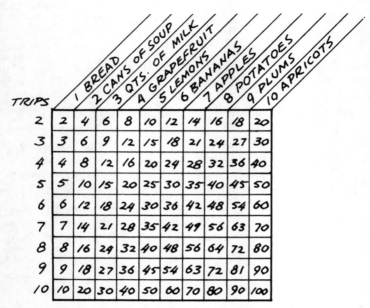

Figure 21A: *A multiplication chart based on trips to the store.*

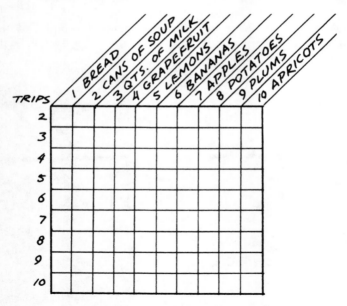

Figure 21B: *The same chart left blank to be filled in by a child.*

126

division is the reverse of multiplication; that the number we need at the top is the one that, when multiplied by the one on the left, gives us the number on the right. (Does he know *left* and *right*?)

When Flavius gains skill at short division, teach him – or have tutors teach him – long division. The teaching of long division, of decimals, percentages, fractions, angles and degrees can be easily be handled by the tutors if you supply them with an inexpensive paperback dealing with basic arithmetic, perhaps *Mathematics Made Simple*.

12

Innovative Challenges

Up to this point we have dealt with subjects that have traditionally formed the cornerstone of education: the three R's – reading, 'riting, and 'rithmatic. When these subjects are taught at an early age, to preschoolers rather than school-age children, the result is a bonus of high intelligence, as we have repeatedly seen. But there are other, non-academic, ways to generate intellectual growth for young children. Three, in daily use at the Ledson Institute, add a remarkable power to children's mind. Time to consider them.

May the Force Be with You

My constant mention that certain activities require effort on your child's part draws attention to the frequently overlooked trait that distinguishes those who lead in any field from those who follow. I am speaking of pluck: the quality that empowers one person to pursue a task doggedly and relentlessly, and to complete it successfully when others would give up. This characteristic – call it perseverance, resoluteness, tenacity or what you will – is the force that gives flower to the various benefits we want children to have. High intelligence – even up to genius level – will accomplish little without determination and purpose. Thomas Edison nailed this truth down when he said, "Genius is one per cent inspiration, ninety-nine per cent perspiration." Unless high education and high intelligence are accompanied by endurance, all you have is a bright dilettante – one who will be left behind by the 'plodding mediocrity'.

The diligent pursuit of a task, its successful completion, the feeling of triumph, and the 'can do' attitude it generates are worth our attention. The best news is that this trait can be nurtured and strengthened. To accomplish this goal we present children with a simple task, then gradually increase its difficulty until – to everyone's surprise – young children demonstrate remarkable endurance and achieve remarkable accomplishments (see page 140). The self-confidence arising from this exercise permits children to deal stoically with challenges they encounter now, and later as an adult. True grit.

A particularly effective grit-boosting activity at the Institute is the solving of mazes.

Mazes

Children begin with a very simple maze, as seen in Maze 1, and asked to draw a line from the mouse to the cheeses and to do so without touching the grid lines. Depending on a child's age, he or she may have to be shown how to do this. Children gradually advance to more difficult mazes and their self-esteem rises with each successive triumph.

The activity provokes thought and diligence and provides still one more benefit: practice in manipulating a writing tool: valuable preparation for eventual printing and writing.

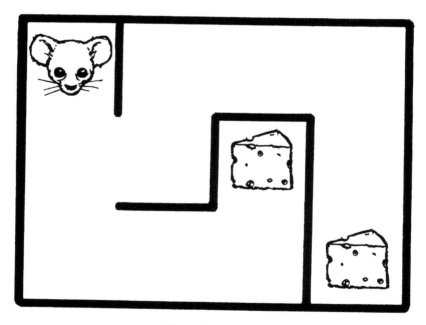

Figure 23: *Maze 1.*

Preparation of the Mazes

Make two photocopies of Maze 1. Remove a different cheese from each copy with white-out. Now you have two different mazes. Photocopy the two altered mazes in whatever quantity you think you will need. Present the first maze to your child, Ernst, and ask him to draw a line from the mouse to the cheese. Depending on his age, you might have to show him what is required. By having Ernst tackle the same maze several times, he will become familiar with what is required while gaining control over the pencil. You might have to enlarge the size of the mazes to help him avoid touching the lines. When Ernst can solve both versions of Maze 1 easily, move on to Maze 2.

Figure 24: *Alex Hung, age five, excelled in solving mazes. See his solution to the maze on page 140.*

Repeat the same procedure with Maze 2 and with all the others mazes. Photocopy each maze as many times as there are cheeses shown on it; then, on each maze, white out all but one cheese – a different one – on each photocopy. Then photocopy your doctored copies to create

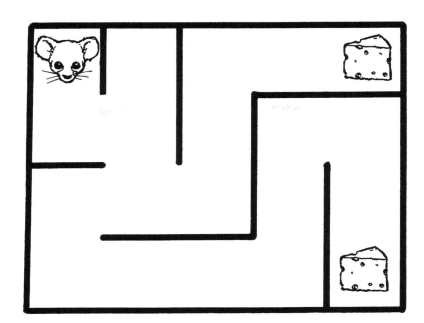

Maze 2

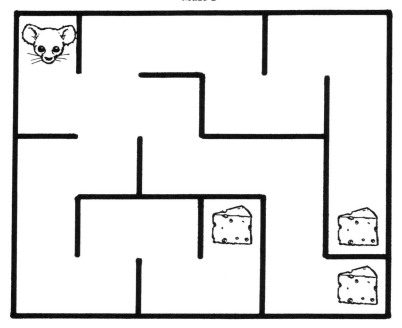

Maze 3

131

more copies for Ernst to work with. Though only ten mazes are included in the book, you will be able to create thirty-six difference mazes by this method. Make sure Ernst tackles the easiest version of each maze first.

You will have to enlarge some of the mazes to help Ernst avoid crossing lines. How much you enlarge them will depend on the age of your child and his or her ability to control a pencil.

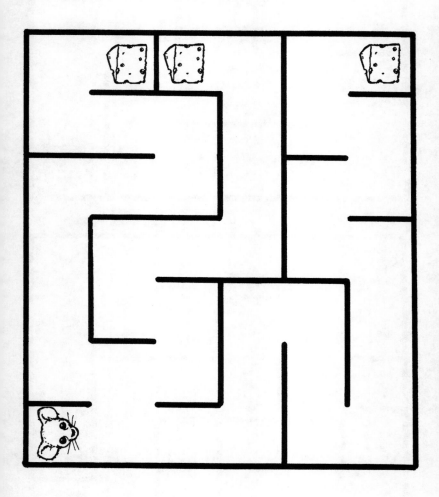

Maze 4

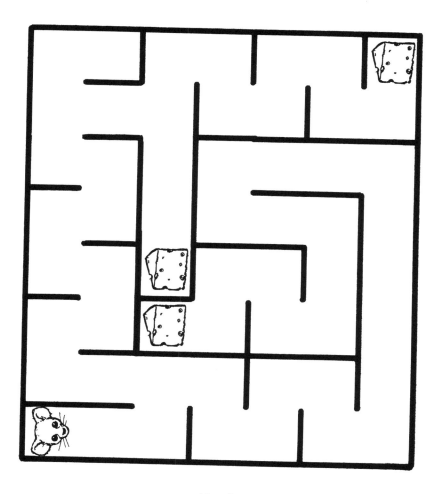

Maze 5

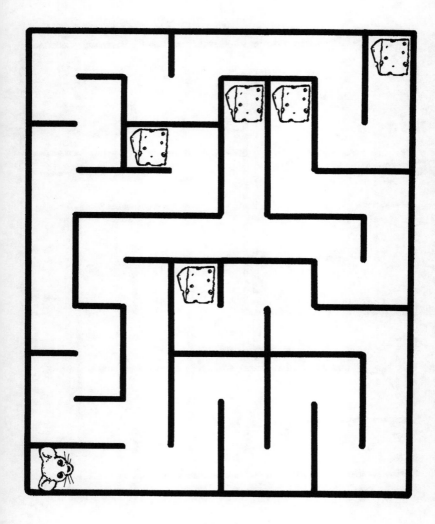

Maze 6

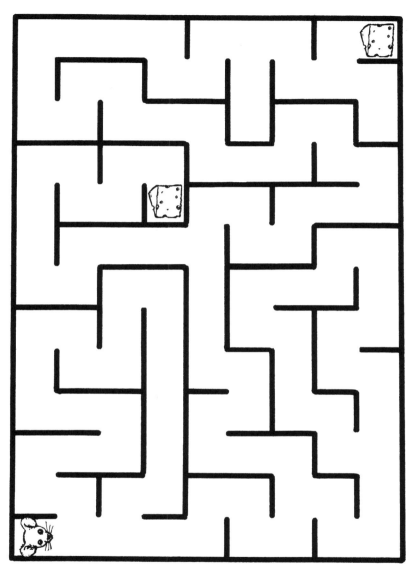

Maze 7

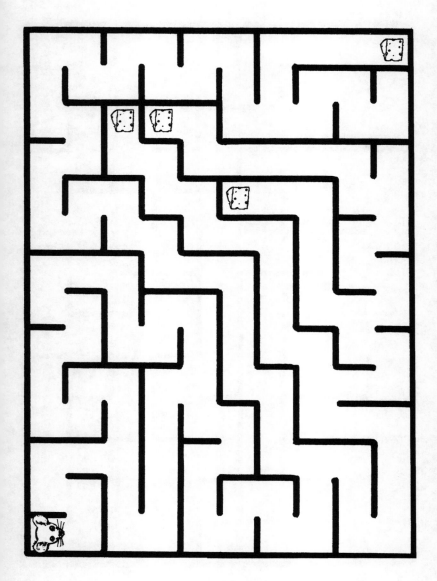

Maze 8

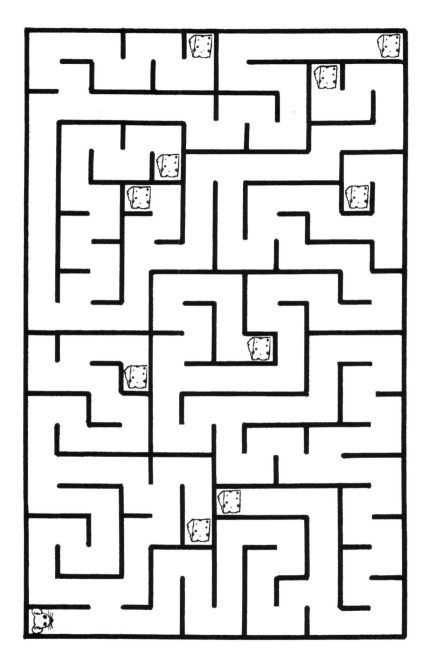

Maze 9

Maze 10

To see how Alex Hung solved this maze, turn the page.

A five-year-old triumphs!

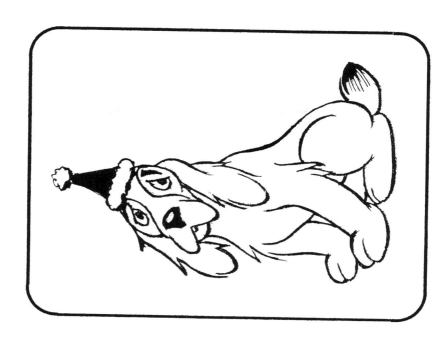

Figure 26: *The Diligent Spotter: a simple challenge with six differences.*

Figure 27: *The Diligent Spotter: an advanced challenge with eight differences.*

The Diligent Spotter

This is the name we have given to an activity that advances visual acuity and, of course, perseverance. You have probably seen examples of this playful exercise on the entertainment pages for children in a newspaper. Two pictures are shown; but they differ in several small ways and children are expected to find as many of the changes as they can.

We have created a series of these puzzles, beginning with very simple ones that gradually become more difficult. You can easily make your own collection of puzzles at home. Here's how.

Clip a simple drawing – not a photograph – from a magazine or newspaper and make two photocopies, enlarging it if appropriate. Alter one of the photocopies in several ways with whiteout and pen, then photocopy the result. Present the altered photocopy and the untouched photocopy to Ernst and let him find the differences.

Begin with simple problems, as shown on page 141. Ernst will gradually develop keen visual perception; being eventually able to work with advanced versions of the sort shown on page 142.

But caution: Keep the changes laughably simple and obvious at first. If your youngster doesn't easily see the changes, he may lose interest and a valuable exercise would be doomed before it got started. Advance slowly, always keeping your child's success foremost in mind. Oh, and don't forget to give loud praise when he spots the differences.

Memory

The rewards of having a good memory are many. Fortunately, we can improve your child's ability to remember with another game. At the Institute, five or six silhouettes are shown to the children. After a moment or two, the cards are put away. A few minutes later each child is given a sheet of paper showing twenty-five silhouettes and asked to circle which silhouettes were displayed earlier. As children become practiced in remembering, you can gradually lengthen the lapse of time and increase the number of images shown. Eventually, Safina Allidina, seen next page, was able to remember thirteen symbols out of thirteen shown when tested *three days later.*

You can easily construct your own set of cards. Paste photos or draw shapes on pieces of card stock – perhaps on the back of old business cards Your collection could be a mixture of faces, symbols, tools, numbers, letters, animals – almost anything you wish. You needn't start with as many as twenty-five.

For the test sheet, photocopy smaller versions of each picture or design. Glue these smaller versions on a piece of typing paper and make copies of it.

Figure 28: *Safina Allidina, age six, shown performing the Ledson Memory Energizer test, was able to read at a Grade 8 level.*

Start simply. The age of your child will dictate the level of challenge at which you begin. Bear in mind that it will take time just for Ernst to understand what is required of him. Begin by showing him two or three of the original photos. You might comment briefly on each. Then put the cards away and give Ernst a test sheet. Ask him to circle the pictures he saw earlier.

The activity can be made easier by reducing the length of time between viewing and his marking, or made more difficult by increasing the number of items shown, or increasing the length of time before he is asked to mark the items viewed. Make a note on his test page of the number of items he remembered and the number you showed him, and the lapse of time before he was asked to remember them. With repeated practice you will see impressive advancement. One parent reported of his youngster, "He remembers conversations and discussions with enviable recollection of what was said and done, by who, and where."

You can add sparkle to the exercise by marking a test sheet for the puppet who whispers in your ear his recollection of the items previously shown. Of course, he gets them all wrong.

Jigsaw puzzles promote a tenacity of purpose and are popular with even our two-year-olds. Begin with simple puzzles – fewer than a dozen pieces – and gradually introduce more complex puzzles. Whether or not Ernst wants to continue with more difficult puzzles will depend to some extent on the fuss and celebration you make when he completes a demanding task. *Lay it on thick!*

The game of checkers provokes thought, and if the dummy whispers in your ear silly moves for you to make, you can be sure Ernst will laughingly win every time. Building blocks present a challenge in construction while promoting precise hand movement. In building a teetering tower, children face a worthy problem. If the tower crumbles, they are motivated to try again.

I have seen a youngster work earnestly for days trying to solve the puzzle shown at Figure 29. The challenge is to draw a continuous line that crosses each vertical and horizontal leg once and once only. Below it, a failed attempt with an X on the uncrossed section.

Toy stores contain a variety of challenging activities. Visit one and stock up.

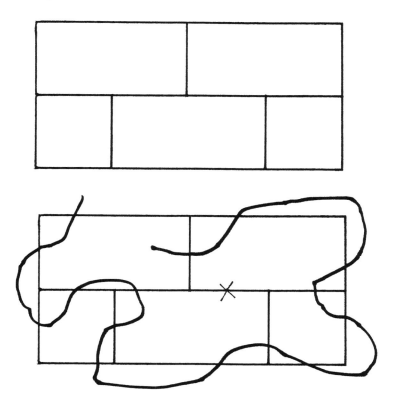

Figure 29: *A low-cost, challenging problem.*

13

Advanced Knowledge and Skills

When a child asks where pomegranates grow, or the distance to the moon, or what worms eat, the response, "I don't know," is an educational dead-end unless it is followed by "Let's find out." The youngster who can read but who hasn't yet learned how information is alphabetically indexed remains dependent upon his parent for locating information quickly. The purpose of this chapter is to equip children with advanced knowledge and skills that will extend their ability to gather information and thus fit them for a continuing program – for a lifelong program! – of self-education.

Indexing

A major advance is achieved when a child learns to understand the process we call indexing. This is not difficult to teach. Take nine cards (the backs of old business cards will do) and print a word on each: *ant, arm, ash, bat, big, bus, cat, cot,* and *cup*. Turn the cards facedown and mix them up. Print a single letter on three other cards: **A** on one, **B** on a second, and **C** on the third. Place these three cards side by side to form headings for three columns you will be creating. Have your child, Firoz, turn over one of the nine face-down word cards and place it beneath the card having the same letter the word begins with, **A**, **B**, or **C**. He then turns over another card and, again, positions it beneath the card bearing its beginning letter. Turning over another, Firoz positions it appropriately and continues in this manner until all nine cards have been correctly positioned.

Now take the three cards under **A**, *ant, arm,* and *ash*. Tell Firoz to notice the second letter in each word and ask him to tell you when he hears you speak one of the three letters, an **N**, an **R**, or an **S**. Slowly recite the alphabet. When you get to **N**, Firoz may notice that **N** is the second letter in *ant*. (Then again, he may not. This is a difficult task.) If he doesn't notice, draw his attention to the **N** and position the card topmost in the word column beneath the letter **A**. Continue reciting the alphabet from **N**. When you get to **R**, the second letter in *arm*, Firoz may not notice the fact. Indeed, he still may not even be clear of what he is expected to do. Position the word *arm* beneath *ant*, and continue your recitation to **S** for *ash*. Point out him what is now obvious (obvious, that is, to you and me) and place the card beneath *arm*.

Turn the nine word-cards facedown, mix them, and have Firoz repeat the procedure. He will begin to see that in placing the words appropriately in the **A** column, the second letter is now almost as important as the first letter. When he can detect the correct sequence of cards for the **A** column as you recite the alphabet, apply the same procedure to the three cards in the **B** column. When Firoz can sequence words correctly for the **A** and **B** columns, proceed with the final three words, *cat, cot,* and *cup*, for the **C** column.

Firoz will begin to see the link between the way words are spelled and the way they are sorted. A week or two later, when he is brimming with confidence, add nine more word cards to the exercise: *and, art, ask, bag, bit, bus, can, cob,* and *cut*. When, finally, Firoz can easily position the eighteen words in the correct order, draw his attention to the third letter in each word. Some of the words in each row will be, by chance, already positioned correctly by virtue of their third letter. If not, point out to Firoz the important role now played by the third letter and have him reposition the appropriate cards.

When you have completed this exercise with the eighteen word-cards and Firoz can position them in the order they would appear in a dictionary, he will have made a monumental advance. But be patient. This is a difficult task and he may need considerable guidance. When this procedure is clear in his head, show him how he can use this information to play a game. The game is Bargain Hunting, and you will need a mail-order catalog.

To begin, establish certain pages in the catalog as being 'bargain' pages. These can be any pages you wish; perhaps every page that is divisible by five, or pages having a 1, or, 2 or 3 in their page-numbers. Having established that much, the first player – let's say it's you – names some item that is probably in the catalog – perhaps, *towels*. Firoz then checks the index in the catalog to see what page the towels are on. If towels are on a page that was established as a bargain page, you gain a point or a treat; perhaps a cornflake or a raisin. Now it is Firoz's turn. He chooses *soap*, then checks the index to see if soap is situated on a bargain page. You probably get the idea now. By continuing in this way, and letting Firoz check each item, he will gain skill in using the index.

Another exercise in indexing is to have Firoz locate the names of friends and relatives in the telephone directory.

Finally, prompt Firoz to find specific words in the dictionary. Unaided, he may take four or five minutes – perhaps even longer – to locate each word. This is hard work for a youngster, so be sure to explode with compliment for his every success.

Grammar, Salted and Peppered with Humor

Many years ago when I was a captive at Pape Avenue Public School in the east end of Toronto, teachers taught grammar. Well, that's not quite right. They *dispensed* grammar, mouthing indecipherable concepts about parts of speech with no concern that their meaning wasn't getting across. Does the term *subjective completion* mean anything to you? It didn't mean much to me at age twelve. If pupils could decipher this bafflegab, fine; otherwise, you had to repeat a year, as some of us did.

A study of grammar might be thought too advanced for inclusion here, but young Firoz may want to put his thoughts on paper some day and it would be nice if he could do so correctly. Moreover, there is a special need because if *you* don't teach him basic grammar, he may not learn it. Grammar is seldom taught in schools today. We can't blame teachers for not knowing what they themselves haven't been taught. Grammar has always been purveyed in a complicated, humorless, and unimaginative way. The names of the verb forms alone – transitive, intransitive and copula – have anesthetic power.

The first barrier to understanding grammar lies in its special vocabulary. Just as the motor in your car has its unique parts – *carburetor, distributor, piston, cylinder, valve*, and so on – grammar has its own parts: *noun, pronoun, verb, adjective, adverb, preposition, conjunction,* and *interjection (*or *exclamation)*. Knowing these names doesn't equip us to speak with precision; it merely lets us discuss language usage in a way that is universally understood. When an auto mechanic tells you the spark plugs are fouled, and the distributor points are worn, you have an idea (or maybe you haven't) of what he is talking about. By understanding the parts of grammar, Firoz will be able to discuss English usage with a language mechanic – otherwise known as a scholar or knowledgeable teacher.

Long after I left school, I discovered that grammar was easy to understand when it was expressed in simpler terms. So, let's start slowly.

148

A *noun* is something you can see, hear, smell, feel, taste or discuss, *curtains, beauty, clouds, perfume, impatience, puzzlement, ketchup.* Any word that will fit into the sentence, *"Let's talk about (a, an, the).....*" is a noun. A noun is considered singular or plural depending on whether it represents one item or more than one item. *Man* is singular, *men* is plural. *Woman* is singular, *women* is plural. A noun is called a *proper noun* if it has a capital letter: *Terry Fox, Philadelphia, Orange Bowl, Earth.* Most other nouns are *common nouns*; items such as *native, district, tower, paper, wall.*

A *pronoun* is a word that stands-in. In Hollywood, stand-ins are important on movie sets. Instead of making the star stand immobile in position while technicians adjust the lights, camera and sound equipment, the stand-in takes on this work. In a similar way, pronouns stand-in for nouns. Here's how. Take the sentence, "Sam jumped up because he was angry." Here, Sam is a noun. In fact, it's a proper noun. The word *he* (which is standing in for Sam) is a stand-in – a pronoun. If we didn't have pronouns we would have to keep repeating the noun, "Sam jumped up because Sam was angry," which could become tedious. Some frequently used pronouns are *he, she, it, him, her, me, us, we, they,* and *them.*

An *adjective* tells us more about a noun. It's a describing word. To illustrate, *day* is a noun. But what sort of day is it – *hot, cold, warm, clear, snowy, rainy, dark, windy*? These are various words we use to describe the day. They are noun-describers. They are adjectives.

A *verb* is the motor in a sentence. It tells us what is happening or what state exists. *One clear days we used to throw rocks off the cliff.* Is there any action in this sentence? Yes, there is some throwing going on. So *throw* is a verb. Now, the business gets a little stickier. There are two verb forms we need to know. One is called a *transitive* verb. The *trans* part of this word suggests action and distance – as in the words *trans*continental and *trans*port. To just say, *We used to throw*, doesn't make sense. Something has to be thrown. What was it? Rocks. The throwing had to act on something – that's the *trans* part. So *throwing* is an active verb. It's transitive.

Another type of verb is called an *intransitive* verb. If you suspected this verb wasn't active, you'd be right. *On sunny days we used to sing.* This makes sense without adding more words. *Sing* is intransitive. Of course we might tell where we sang, how we sang, or what we sang – hymns, folk songs, the national anthem – but these words aren't required. The sentence makes sense as it stands.

Verbs have what are called tenses. Two verb tenses will suit our needs for the moment: present tense and past tense. A few present tense verbs are *see, hear, try*, and *look*. Their past tenses are *saw, heard, tried,* and *looked*.

An *adverb* adds information to a verb. (Adjectives, you'll remember, add information only to nouns.) Adverbs are describers telling us where, when, why, how, and to what extent something is done. To illustrate, were the rocks thrown *quickly, accurately, clumsily, skillfully, forcefully?* Did we sing *all day, intermittently, loudly, off key?* Adverbs are sometimes easy to spot because they often end with *ly*.

A *preposition* tells us the relationship that exists between a noun and some other word in a sentence. *Into, on, around, beside, near, between,* are prepositions. In our sample sentence above, rocks were thrown. Where were they thrown and what is the relationship between *rocks* and *cliff?* Were the rocks thrown *into* the cliff? *Onto* the cliff? *Through* the cliff? Obviously not. These prepositions are unsuitable. The preposition we need is *off* the cliff.

Conjunctions can join words, parts of a sentence, or whole sentences. Here are a few: *and, but, if, whether, however, therefore, where, why*.

Interjections are merely gasps or exclamations: *Oh! My! Holy Moley!*

Enough. Admittedly, there is more to be learned about grammar than this, but the purpose here is merely to give you courage to continue studying the subject on your own. Now, the game.

The Grammar Game

Until Rosa clearly understands the workings of the game and the grammatical terms used, it would be best if *you* played the dominant role in the game. Begin by writing a sentence on paper; perhaps, *Jack be nimble, Jack be quick; Jack jump over the candlestick.* Rosa isn't to know what you have written. You then ask her to provide words to fill a precise grammatical role in the sentence, beginning, perhaps, with a proper noun. (You will remember that proper nouns usually have a capital letter. You may have to help her.) Suppose she suggests *Prince Charles.* You would strike out the three proper nouns in your written text – *Jack* – and replace them with *Prince Charles.* Next, you might ask for two adjectives that describe people. She might suggest *beautiful* and *hairy.* You would strike out the adjectives *nimble* and *quick* and insert *beautiful* and *hairy.* By successively requesting an intransitive verb (in the present tense), a preposition, and a common noun (singular) to replace *jump, over,* and *candlestick.* Let's say she suggests *fly, into,* and *wallpaper.* You could now finish your alterations. Read aloud the sentence as you first wrote it: *Jack be nimble, Jack be quick; Jack jump over the candlestick,* then read Rosa's revised version of it: *Prince Charles be beautiful, Prince Charles be hairy; Prince Charles fly into the wallpaper.*

Children sometimes convulse into fits of giggles when playing the game – which can be made funnier still by involving family members or friends. For example, *Uncle Andrew and Aunt Debbie visited Niagara Falls in the trailer* can become comical if the relative's names are left intact. One possible result: *Uncle Andrew and Aunt Debbie shouted Mickey Mouse in their golf ball.*

Start your games by changing only the nouns. When Rosa gains a clear understanding of nouns, add pronouns, and gradually add the other parts of speech. You might eventually purchase an inexpensive grammar workbook to advance this basic knowledge.

Composition

You don't have to be a writer to teach Rosa to write. A little instruction and plenty of practice will work marvels. We will consider two forms of writing: fictional writing and factual writing.

Encouraging children to write fiction exercises their imagination; and imagination triggers innovation and inventiveness: both highly prized characteristics. You can find plot ideas for stories in several ways. You might ask Rosa to compose a chain of words; each word beginning with the letter that the previous word ended with. For example, suppose she suggests *cat* for her first word. Her next word must begin with a **T**; perhaps *tomato*. Now, her next word must begin with an **O**. In this way, Rosa's chain of plot words might become *cat-tomato-owl-lake-elephant*. Next, she composes sentences, each of which contains a plot word. Then by stringing her sentences together as a story, she might end up with something like this.

> A cat named Harold lived in the country. Harold didn't eat mice, but he loved tomatoes. One day, while he was eating a juicy tomato, an owl hooted. Harold thought the hoot was the sound of a boat on the nearby lake. He raced down to the wharf to have a chat with the captain, a friend of his who happened to be an elephant.

Nonsense is, of course, essential if the exercise is to charm children.

Another device for creating simple plot ideas is the 'fortunately-unfortunately' method in which statements alternately express fortunate and unfortunate events. Here is a ghastly tale that will delight most children.

One day the Queen of Zazu dyed her hair blond.

Unfortunately, her hair fell out.

Fortunately, her eyebrows and eyelashes stayed in place.

Unfortunately, her ears dropped off the following week.

Fortunately, her hair grew back in and hid the space where her ears had been.

Unfortunately, the new hair was blue in color.

Rosa might then be shown how each of the plot lines could be enlarged and extra sentences added to make a more interesting story. For example.

> *One day, Her Majesty the Queen of Zazu decided she would like to dye her hair blonde. But when the Queen applied the dye to her hair, it fell out. Luckily, her eyelashes and eyebrows stayed in place.*
>
> *A week later, while trying to put on an earring, the ear came off in her fingers. The other dropped off shortly after lunch. A few days later, her hair grew back in. But it was blue.* [Occasionally, the King of Zazu asks the Queen to dye her hair a different color, but she has no ears for his suggestion.]

Another captivating source of writing material is presented by *Let's Pretend*. Rosa might pretend to be a doctor or a veterinarian, then describe some services she performed during the day; how she treated an elephant's runny nose, an alligator's toothache, a lion's dandruff. Similarly, she might recount her adventures as a policewoman, a nurse, a detective, or as the captain of a ship.

Children delight in writing stories that grant them unusual powers.

Here are four suggested themes. You might think of others.

> *What I'd do if I were invisible.*
>
> *What I'd do if I had a million dollars.*
>
> *What I'd do if I had the strength of ten people.*
>
> *What I'd do if I could float in the air.*

Factual Writing

Writing reports from encyclopedia entries – suitable for an older child – provides a doubly educative step to writing. You might simplify the steps given here until Rosa gains ease and speed in composing reports for her *Encyclopedia Report Book.* Explain the procedure in words she understands.

1. Read the entry on some topic in the encyclopedia.

2. Read the entry again. This time, write on separate slips of paper a word, two, or three, mentioning important points,

3. Put the encyclopedia away. Arrange the slips in whatever order you wish – which can be different from the order the details were mentioned in the encyclopedia.

4. Expand the notes into sentences and join these sentences together on another piece of paper. This is called an outline.

5. Rewrite the outline, expanding on each point mentioned. The result is called a first draft.

6. Read the draft. Mark corrections and additions. Check the spelling and grammar.

7. Write the finished report.

Rosa might start with reports of only twenty or thirty words, gradually increasing their length as she gains confidence. Of course, she should choose the topics that she wants to write about.

14

Chance Education

Until now, we have dealt with matters clearly seen to raise your child's intelligence. But there are other matters, seen less clearly, that can thwart that advancement. The everyday haphazard guidance your child encounters, or is likely to encounter – random ambient instruction – can reinforce your good guidance or, more frequently, thwart its effectiveness. The uninvited, unregulated and uncontrolled education a child receives without parental consent or approval deserves attention. Television provides one rich source of unregulated guidance. A second influential source is provided by the children your child encounters. We'll begin with television.

TV, Siren of the Airwaves

"Come, look at me. I'm colorful, beautiful, entertaining – and free." If TV sets could talk, that might be their message. In truth, television isn't free. The cost is time, and sometimes it's a heavy cost, particularly among children. Most children's pastimes – reading, playing games, engaging in hobbies, and so on – channel away a mere trickle of time, but TV sluices away a torrent of time – reportedly more than twenty hours a week

Whether we wish it or not, TV is a major educating force in most children's lives. The benefits and malignancies of TV, and their influence on children's conduct and attitude are suitable material for an entire book, but we must keep this comment brief.

Violence

Almost any page in a TV guide presents a panorama of crime ranging from simple discourtesy to repugnant acts. The ultimate price? More than 2,000 studies have shown an indisputable link between TV violence and the frequency of real-life crimes. In this way, vicious acts depicted on TV extend their malevolent power.

154

The antisocial behavior fostered by television is a natural legacy of the bent people who inhabit the world of the picture tube. The collective television 'family' is disproportionately stocked with neurotics and cutthroats. The prevalence of thugs in the real world runs to one percent of the population; however, crooks compose seventeen per cent of all televised characters. If seventeen percent of your neighbors were crooks, you might be on the phone to the movers pretty quick. Worse, TV brings the rogues right into your living room.

The distorted representation of humanity seen on television afflicts children with what has been termed the 'mean world syndrome'. Researchers report that the more television children watch, the more fearful, anxious, and suspicious they become of the world around them, and the more likely they are to condone aggressive behavior in themselves and in others. The message conveyed is *Get them before they get you!* and *Guns solve arguments quicker!* Murder is so common that unless it is executed in a sufficiently imaginative or outrageous manner it hardly holds the attention of a connoisseur.

Children are particularly vulnerable to the influence of antisocial acts seen on television because they haven't the immense backlog of personal experiences to affirm that while unsavory events do occur in daily life they don't occur with anywhere near the frequency enacted on television.

The greatest crime – and it's surreptitious – is the stunting influence television inflicts on imagination and creativity: losses for which television may eventually be most loudly damned. Public school teachers report that some children are unable to understand stories that aren't illustrated. Television is seen to rob children of the ability to form pictures clearly in their mind.

TV has been found to exert an adverse influence on perseverance – the ability to stick at a task and complete it. Accustomed to seeing every problem resolved in thirty to sixty minutes on television, children develop a low tolerance for difficulties faced when learning. Projects that require diligence for their solution are apt to be avoided and, if undertaken, they are often abandoned as soon as a complication is encountered. Teachers lament the way children dissolve into tears if a task *looks* hard.

Palate Tickling

Television greatly influences eating habits, clearly seen by the prevalence of fat children. Until the 1940s, the only overweight children were those with a glandular problem. The wide promotion of junk foods

– low in nutrition, high in fat and sugar – encourages high caloric intake, which, of course, promotes obesity.

Television Allurement

Television is said to have redeeming educational qualities. *National Geographic, Nova,* and similar programs devoted to nature are sometimes hailed by educators as exciting new ways to fill the obligations of school outside the classroom – so thought the former U.S. Commissioner of Education, Ernest Boyer, when he said,

> *It* [TV] *has caused children to travel around the world. They've gone to the bottom of the ocean, to the top of the greatest mountain…and we've seen the moon, and we've looked at Earth from outer space.*

We have indeed. But, as newspaper reports constantly attest, it hasn't done much for literacy. If children are led to believe that visually opulent television presentations are acceptable substitutes for learning basic academic skills, these visual feasts come at a high price. Moreover, the rich color and sound, the musical accompaniment, and sometimes highly literate narration, can overwhelm the senses; but they often convey little important information. Then there's a two-way stretch. A few feet of instructional film can be artfully stretched into a lengthy program by including extraneous diversions the mesmerized viewer won't question. It may seem incomprehensible to parents of this high-tech generation to hear that children were better educated before the advent of electronic gadgetry. It's a fact.

A point frequently overlooked is that television can be *mis*educational. In any filmed recreation of events, truth is rarely allowed to spoil an entertaining story. Bending the truth is a Hollywood tradition. One saw a movie for entertainment then read the book to find out what really happened. But children watch so much television they often haven't time for reading. And that brings us to the final grievous complaint regarding television.

Hidden Costs

In the final assessment, the greatest evil attributable to television may not be the impairments that can be measured or even observed, but the unobserved childhood activities that get squeezed out of a youngster's life simply because television leaves scant time for them. This would include playing games, working out puzzles, collecting stamps, coins, minerals or rocks, building model toys and other contrivances, reading, or learning to play a musical instrument.

Another peril of too much television viewing is its stifling influence on family communication. In some homes television dominates much of the conversation, family members being allowed to chat only during the commercials.

But now, the most overlooked and subtle cost of TV viewing is, for children, the instant escape it provides from boredom. But boredom provides a mysterious power in a child's life. Boredom detonates enterprise. Boredom prompts thought, fires imagination, and encourages resourcefulness. And resourcefulness is the same metal from which inventiveness is forged.

Yet, in examining the trees, we may miss the woods. Perhaps the most pernicious element of television is the insidious way it turns youngsters into viewers by habit. When children enter Grade 1, having by that time watched an estimated four thousand hours of television, they are well habituated to television's fascinating spell. Can we really expect six-year-olds to suddenly kick the habit of a *lifetime* to accommodate school and social activities? During their week with no television, some children at Friend's Central Public School reacted as addicts do when suddenly deprived of a hard drug. They begged, cried and screamed for television and tried to figure ways around the ban they had pledged to honor. Is it any better with adults? In Germany, 184 volunteers were paid to give up television for a year. None made it past six months.

Though heavily committed television viewers would find it difficult to believe, life *does* go on without television. Indeed, in some homes where the television set has been banished, life seems to go on in an exceptionally pleasant way. One San Francisco father decided he wouldn't replace the television set when it broke down. His five sons, rebellious and resentful at first, championed the father's decision later. They became involved in sports, Sea Scouts, tap dancing, and reading, and developed a range of interests far wider than most children their age.

Peer Influence

Your child is likely to display the qualities prevalent in your home. His manners, speech, ethics, and attitude toward learning will be those you have demonstrated and nurtured. And, of course, the children your child plays with will exhibit the attitudes, qualities, and aspirations that prevail in their homes. Every child therefore becomes a perambulating model of his home environment. In this roundabout way, other parents

157

impress their values on your child through their children. This is fine so long as their values, priorities and goals agree with your own. But you can't count on it. Consider; how many people do you meet who share your enthusiasm for early education, quality speech, and scrupulous manners?

> *"The hardest job kids face today is learning good manners without seeing any."*
> Fred Astaire

Parents can control the youngsters their children will play with when they are near home, and it is wise that they do so. But control is lost when their child enters a daycare center.

Day Care Centers

Institutionalized childcare provides the second great source of chance learning. And, as we will see, it's risky.

The mass surrender of early childhood management to those outside the family is a fairly recent practice. Until the 1940s mothers stayed home with their young. Today, most mothers work outside the home and their children are reared in a daycare center. This exacts a price. Two, in fact. The first affects the parent-child relationship.

A team at Michael Reese Hospital in Chicago examined 110 one-year-olds from affluent families. Half of the infants received parental care; the other half received care from stable, hired caretakers. Youngsters in the second group were seen to develop a less secure relationship with their mothers, a finding corroborated by a similar study in Michigan which found that one-year-olds in full-time daycare demonstrated a greater avoidance of their mothers than did those reared by their parent.

The second risk associated with institutionalized care lies in learning anti-social conduct, seen especially among slightly older children. A study of age five- to eight-year-olds who spent their early years at a highly regarded daycare at the University of North Carolina showed the children were more likely to hit, kick, threaten and argue than those who had not attended day care or who had started later. And still another study near Dallas found daycare children less cooperative and less popular; they had poorer grades and less self-esteem by Grade 3. In spite of the recorded hazards of daycare, the staff at such centers routinely thump the drum for 'peer group interaction' which, in plain language, means learning to get along with others; ignoring, of course, the fact that rough company invites rough response.

Learning to get along with others is assuredly important, but the traits that win ready acceptance and friendship with others – kindness, consideration, honesty, gentleness – do not require the presence of a group for their nurture and emergence. Contrary to the message of daycare operators, these winning characteristics become forfeit by membership in an unselected group.

But, if you have little choice in the matter, and must find a responsible care-giving service, how do you go about it?

First, ask around. Find others who leave their children at a day care. Ask them what they think of the service provided. What are its strengths? What are its weaknesses? Wait outside a daycare at the end of the day and quiz parents arriving to pick up their children. (Parents are more likely to have a moment to talk at night than in the morning when hurrying to work.) Do the parents you speak to have concerns similar to your own?

When you arrange to visit a daycare center, have someone accompany you. Four eyes are better than two, and two minds are better than one. Your companion might think of an important question to ask, one you might have missed.

A first concern is your child's physical and emotional well being. Do children at the center seem happy and relaxed – even the smaller ones who might be tyrannized by bigger, stronger children in a poorly managed establishment?

What is the child-to-caregiver ratio? An unethical operator can present plausible excuses for 'temporary' large ratios. Some operators are not averse to pressing the cook, bookkeeper, or janitor into the momentary role of teacher to give the appearance of a low ratio while visitors are present.

Are there plenty of play materials for the children, and have they any educating value? Parents might be impressed by the great range of toys and their new appearance, failing to notice that the toys are on shelves too high for the children to reach. Are there first-aid materials? Does anyone know how to use them? Are fire drills held regularly? When was the last one?

If a noon meal is served, is the menu posted for the day? Might you examine the menus for the past week or for the next week? Bear in mind that a menu can provide a deceptive description of the meal that ends up in front of a child, and with only your child to witness what is served, you may never know whether the lunch measured up to its description unless you visit while the children are eating.

How are children disciplined? How are anti-social acts suppressed?

The reason for listing these cautions is not to show that most caregivers are bandits, but rather to show that daycare presents easy opportunities for deception. Claims made for extended program activities are sometimes overblown or non-existent.

Perhaps the riskiest way to select a daycare is to make a decision based on its advertising. Slick promotion can be gulling. And, mention of misrepresentation raises – strangely enough – the name Montessori. Maria Montessori, the pioneer of intellectual advancement, would be horrified to see how freely her name is falsely used to attract business. The name Montessori is not protected by copyright, so anyone can start a child minding service, call it a Montessori school, and ignore the program for which that grand lady is famous. This means you must carefully judge each Montessori school on its observable features, not on its name.

When your child reaches age six, the law states he must attend a school unless you are able to, and prepared to, provide an acceptable program of instruction at home. This matter is dealt with in the next chapter. But first, a closing note: children are not obliged to attend kindergarten. Schools don't broadcast this information because reduced attendance reduces their income.

15

Public School Education

Several years ago I was asked to address a group of brilliant Grade 6 and 7 children at Churchill Heights Public School, in Toronto. These youngsters, bused daily from various areas of Scarborough (now part of Metropolitan Toronto), engaged in a highly advanced educational program. Entry was limited to children having IQs of at least 140.

My talk dealt with how I went about writing a book. This was before the advent of computers so I explained how continuity of text was achieved by gluing typewritten pages into long strips running perhaps ten or more feet in length. On completing my talk, and incidental to my topic, I asked the children how many had been able to read before they started school. Every hand shot up.

Here, I saw, was corroboration of Dolores Durkin's findings: that children who are able to read before they enter school continue to be the leaders.

The second obvious point was this: the children's parents, not schoolteachers, had generated the youngsters' brilliance. Each parent had given time and effort to equip their child with early advanced abilities. And it had paid off!

Your child will begin school in kindergarten or, if you wait a year (and don't forget, you have the choice), in Grade 1. Kindergarten is a carefree time for children no matter what their academic achievements. And Grade 1 is hardly less so. The child who has benefited from the program in this book may enter Grade 1 with skills at the Grade 5, 6, or 7 level. This isn't likely to create a problem because much of the day in kindergarten and the junior grades is given to activities that appeal to all children regardless of their abilities. There are the morning exercises, show and tell, singing, story time, TV presentations, art, music, crafts, safety talks, hygiene, nature, and any of several other subjects the teacher might introduce.

Children who can read will, of course, notice their advantage over others. But Grade 1 children are usually divided into three or four groups. Those children who can read – and an increasing number *can* read when they start school – simply form their own group. They read while the others are learning how.

If your child, let's call him Julius, is able to read and compute, he will have an academic edge over his classmates. I have seen this turned to a social advantage; for, an advanced child is then able to help other children with their work.

Children taught at home who haven't been allowed – or worse, encouraged – to form a grand opinion of themselves because of their early knowledge and skills, and whose training stressed consideration and respect for others, will usually make friends easily in school and elsewhere. More will be said of this in Chapter 18.

Parents have a role to play in forming a friendly relationship with the teacher. Not all parents observe this nicety. Some have unthinkingly presented their child to the teacher on the first day of school with an attitude of "Lo! My astonishing creation," then tried to wheedle concessions or special attentions for their youngster.

An initial encounter of this sort can spell trouble for parents and children alike. Teachers don't like pushy parents any more than they like pushy children. Though parents are primarily interested in the education of their child, the teacher is more concerned with the education of all thirty in her care. Moreover, bright children can present an unwelcome teaching challenge. The teacher may feel nervous about coping with a bright youngster and perhaps wonder how she will be judged as a result of her performance.

You might alert Julius's teacher to his early achievements without boast or apology in a note:

> *Dear Ms Grey:*
> *Julius has already been taught certain academic matters at home. If you would like to discuss his education at any time, please let me know and I'll be glad to visit you at your convenience.*
> *Yours respectfully,*

Such a note invites friendship. Moreover, it conveys the message that you won't bother the teacher and will remain distant unless she wants to discuss some matter with you.

A sobering note: if Julius attends a public school you can bet he is going to learn as much from his classmates as he will from the teachers.

This opens the sluice gates for uncontrolled, random instruction. The extent of its influence is a gamble; one that John Holt – an educator whose thinking dominated home and school instruction a few years ago – described in this way:

> *If there were no other reason for wanting to keep kids out of school, the social life would be reason enough. In all but a very few of the schools I have taught in, visited, or know anything about, the social life of the children is mean-spirited, competitive, exclusive, status-seeking, snobbish, full of talk about who went to whose birthday party and who got what Christmas presents and who got how many Valentine cards and who is talking to so-and-so and who is not. Even in the first grade, classes soon divide up into leaders (energetic and – often deservedly – popular kids), their bands of followers, and other outsiders who are pointedly excluded from these groups.*
>
> *I remember my sister saying of one of her children, then five, that she never knew her to do anything really mean or silly until she went away to school – a nice school, by the way, in a nice small town.*

Don't expect the principal of even a ghetto school to thump his desktop in emphatic agreement with this sentiment. He isn't likely to acknowledge – even if he secretly believes it – that he is a nominal godfather to numerous rival clans of pink-cheeked warlords.

I have often thought that whereas adults are free to choose their associates, children are thrust into the company of others having manners that adults wouldn't tolerate for a moment.

There is a second risk to public schooling: the quality of instruction. Just from the time Julius enters kindergarten up to the minimum age he might leave school (though he probably wouldn't leave early) he could have twelve or thirteen different teachers. If he (and you) are lucky, all twelve teachers will be knowledgeable, hard-working and dedicated, and Julius will end up well educated. But with that sort of luck, you could make twelve straight passes at a craps table in Las Vegas and end up with a lapful of chips.

> *I never let school interfere with my education.*
> George Bernard Shaw

So, what are you to do? If you think public schooling is too risky, you could send Julius to a private school. Tuition fees must be paid, transportation is another problem, and the pupils aren't necessarily angels. But on the positive side, instruction will probably be better, the supervision tighter, and the curriculum will likely be broader. Private schools are in competition; they must perform well to keep parents happy and stay in business. Public school teachers know better than anyone the uncertainties of public schooling, and they are usually the first to enroll their children in private schools.

There is another option: home schooling. In the 1960s and 70s few dared to risk a school board's wrath by keeping children out of the public school system. Hard-nosed truant officers visited homes sniffing out any detectable or imaginable failing in the home curriculum. Today, home schooling has a wealth of adherents. John Holt ended his career by championing home schooling in his book, *Teach Your Own*, and publishing a periodical, *Growing Without Schooling*, which provided general information on the subject and told parents how to deal with school authorities.

Answering the public outrage over shoddy educational methods and standards, school boards have become much more conciliatory in allowing children to be taught at home.

Home education isn't new. Alexander Graham Bell was taught at home except for one year of private school and two years of high school. Gilbert Grosvenor, long-time editor of *National Geographic,* was taught at home until age ten. General Douglas MacArthur had no formal schooling until he entered West Point whereupon he passed the tests with the highest score ever given an applicant. Franklin D. Roosevelt was taught at home until age fourteen. Yehudi Menuhin had no schooling and Abraham Lincoln was almost wholly self-taught. It seems that with the popularization of home schooling we are returning to a method of education with a proven record of success. Today, more than a million children are being taught wholly at home in North America.

John Holt's home schooling book was written in 1981. Since then an explosion of information has become available through the Internet. You need but type *home schooling* into your search engine to secure complete information on the subject.

As long as you meet the minimal requirements of your local school, you are free to expand upon it and create your own curriculum. Or you could opt for a commercial home program in which everything is designed to win a school board's acceptance. Several are available.

There is still another form of home schooling that entails little financial cost and permits you to create your own curriculum. The program is a mixture of public schooling and home schooling. Let's consider it.

If you have taught Julius throughout his preschool years, you may be reluctant to entrust his continuing education to the public school system. But if you can't stay home each day to teach him, you might follow the example of one enterprising parent who solved this problem in an unusual way. Mr. X sent his children to a public school – but only for a child-minding service – and arranged for young tutors (secured in the manner described in Chapter 5) to continue his program of vocabulary enrichment and mathematics after school and on Saturday mornings. In a venture such as this, we might credit the public school with an educational assist.

Skipping Grades

Let's suppose that, despite your preference for alternative forms of education, Julius must attend public school. Let's further suppose that because his early instruction he enters Grade 1 with abilities comparable to pupils in Grade 4 or 5. Should he skip a grade?

Common sense might indicate that bright pupils should stay with children their own age rather then advance to classes having older children. But studies show this isn't the best course. Researchers have learned that high intelligence is often accompanied by qualities that make grade skipping not only acceptable, but desirable. For example, a link has been found, curiously enough, between intellectual development and physical development; the more intelligent child often being more physically advanced. And the advanced child's emotional and social development are similarly found to be advanced. Super-bright children, therefore, appear to be advanced in everything but age; and age alone is hardly a satisfactory reason for confining a child to the company of those below his or her physical and intellectual level.

A study under the auspices of the State Department of Education, in California, showed that, of 521 children who had been accelerated, only nine experienced serious problems after being placed in higher grades, and these nine had, in fact, been questionable in the first place.

If the principal of Julius's school doesn't want to accelerate him, and he is bored, visit the teacher; tell her you realize she is busy enough coping with so many children – some of whom may be obstreperous or slow to learn – and ask her if you might help keep Julius interested by sending along assignments for him to complete in school. You (or the tutors) would mark Julius's work at home, and send it to the teacher for approval and periodic assessment.

16

Educational Opportunism

We have assessed the chance or random instruction your child might receive from other children and from television. Now let's consider the chance or random opportunities *you* will have to advance your child's knowledge – and consider how you may do so profitably.

During moments when you and young Hermes are together, everything you see and hear can be turned to educational advantage. You need never be lost for something to teach him. Whatever you know that he doesn't know, within reason, is suitable material. His natural curiosity will, of course, prompt him to ask about many matters, but he will ask only about those matters that excite his curiosity. Your role is to direct his attention to, and expand his knowledge of, the objects or topics he overlooks.

Educational opportunism is the practice of seizing any chance occasion to advance your youngster's knowledge of the world around him. In short, by pursuing a program of educational opportunism, you make the world your classroom.

You might begin with matters close to home. The delivery of mail to your door or to the mailbox in the lobby of your building is a convenience of urban life. Does Hermes know that some people are not so fortunate? Why don't people living in the country enjoy this service? Does he know that the purpose of postage stamps isn't decorative, but to prove that payment has been made for delivering the mail? Can he think of a couple of reasons why letters are placed in envelopes before they are dropped into mailboxes? Does he understand the meaning of junk mail? How can manufacturers afford to keep sending unrequested matter when you rarely purchase anything?

Time for lunch: perhaps a can of soup. Why is soup put in cans instead of jars? Why isn't jam put in cans? Does he know that a can of soup is just one tiny portion of an immense batch of soup that was cooked – perhaps enough to feed a thousand people? What are the ingredients in the soup? In fact, what does the word 'ingredients' mean? Does he know that the manufacturer is obliged by law to state the contents of the soup and list its ingredients in the correct order of quantity, the first-named ingredient being the largest component, the last-named being the smallest?

A light bulb burns out. Don't throw it away. Does Hermes know what tungsten is? Put the bulb in a bag and tap it with a hammer. Let him feel the metal and stretch the tiny coils. Does he know that tungsten is also used in toasters and in heating pads and heating blankets?

Many common items around the home can be used to excite a child's interest and thought. And if, occasionally, the enquiry prompts you or Hermes to consult an encyclopedia, then the exercise assumes even greater value.

Shopping trips afford many opportunities for education. First, there is the vocabulary of shopping words: *bargain, discount, merchant, merchandise, guarantee, quality, special* and so on. Teach him these words so he may better understand the world of commerce. At the supermarket, Hermes will have a chance to see, and sometimes touch, unfamiliar items. In the produce department, for example, he might see foods you rarely buy: turnip, watercress, eggplant, leek, and kale.

While shopping, brief side trips to other merchants can add sparkle to your outing. Visit a fish store so he can see lobsters, clams, eels, shrimps and other marine creatures. Regard a department store as you would a museum. Visit the sports department, for example, and introduce Hermes to those exercise or recreational items you don't have at home. Almost any store – the automotive-supply house, the hardware store, the drugstore, and others – can provide educational opportunities. A large shopping mall with its fifty or a hundred adjacent stores is virtually a walk-in encyclopedia of objects to show and explain to him.

Educating Hermes provides an opportunity to advance your own education. Few adults would have the nerve to request an inspection of a merchant's premises. But when the viewing is for a *child*, neither parent nor merchant feels awkward about the request. How many adults have seen the workbench and electronic test equipment in the back of a television and radio repair shop, or the ovens and mixing equipment in the back of a neighborhood bakery, or have examined the tools and machinery with which old shoes are renovated at the shoe repair store? Hermes may be awarded a small souvenir of his visit in the form of a burned-out condenser or resistor, a cookie, or a remnant of leather.

Of course, if all parents imposed on merchants in this way, work would cease in their establishments. However, few parents are sufficiently interested in their children's education – or in their own – to make such a request. Ask your local merchants how many parents have requested an opportunity to let their child look 'out back'. In fact, that question could lead easily to your second question: "Is there a good time of day when it might be possible to let young Felicity here see how you …?" The merchant may simply ask you and Felicity through for an immediate tour.

A walk around the neighborhood can provide its own unique opportunities for rooting out educational truffles. Can you identify different breeds of dogs? Most dog owners will be pleased to tell you the breed and may impart a little information about its care and diet.

Do you know one type of tree from another? The person on whose property a tree stands will likely know its name and will probably be pleased to tell you. How are you at identifying flowers? If you see a flower you can't name, why not ask its owners? They wouldn't have planted the flower unless they liked it, and they'll probably appreciate your interest in the plant. In a similar way, unusual items hanging on porches or in windows justify enquiry.

Will such enquiries arouse resentment? The adage "It's not what you do, it's the way that you do it" comes into play. People don't usually resent a friendly, courteous question – even from a stranger. And accompanied as you are by a youngster, people have little reason to suspect an ulterior motive in your enquiry.

A child serves as a social catalyst, setting a unique situation that permits adults to communicate more easily. For example, while waiting for a bus, a military person in line would probably be pleased to explain to the youngster the significance of his insignias, ribbons, or badges, whereas, were you not accompanied by the child you might not dream of speaking to a stranger.

Traveling with a child provides its own educational opportunities. If you travel by public transit, you can study the passing scene leisurely and point out various interesting objects. If you travel by car and have time to spare you can pull over to observe an attraction, or even turn around and drive back to view something too briefly seen. The expenditure of a mere ten minutes can, in this way, sometimes yield a moment of shared enquiry that will shine long in your memory and in Felicity's too.

Regard each locale as your own special classroom. Let its principal features set the subject. Your cost is one of time. But this needn't be excessive. One family, traveling in United Empire Loyalist country came upon a church built by Americans who crossed Lake Ontario to remain loyal to George III. The plaque read:

HAY BAY CHURCH 1792 –

In 1791, William Losee, an itinerant preacher, organized in this district the first Methodist circuit in

> *Upper Canada. This Meeting House, Upper Canada's first Methodist chapel, was built in 1792. Enlarged in 1834–35 it was used for worship until about 1860 after which it served as a farmer's storehouse. In 1910 in recognition of its historical significance, it was reacquired and restored by The Methodist Church and is still used for annual services by The United Church of Canada.*

Aside from its stock of quaint fact, the text provided words even advanced children might not know. A look inside the church permitted an introduction to the words *pulpit, lectern, gallery*, and *quarrel windows*. The adjoining graveyard contained a stone inscribed: HUFF – IN MEMORY OF PAUL & SOLOMON – UNITED EMPIRE LOYALISTS TRUE TO KING & COUNTRY, which prompted mention of the Boston Tea Party. The total cost of the stop was twenty minutes. But it wasn't the whole reward. Memories count too.

Creating Fond Memories

A program of educational opportunism – or impromptu enquiry, whatever name we might give the practice – will equip Felicity with many broadening experiences. And, as mentioned earlier, they may fill chinks in your own education. But there is more. The main bonus mentioned at the beginning of this chapter comes in creating memorable moments for pleasant recall a year, two, or ten later. Each such learning adventure becomes a bead on a string of rich moments shared with Felicity: "Remember the time when we …?" You will wisely grasp the opportunities of the moment and turn each into a memorable occasion.

Extended Teaching Adventures

Every suggested form of instruction up to this point has been achieved with minimal time or effort. Guidance has been confined to moments of convenience – while you eat, shop, or travel – or left to a time monitored by tutors. However, if you have the time and you wish to contribute further to Felicity's education, there are other interesting ventures you might consider. Here are a few.

The worth of taking children to museums hardly need be mentioned. A common error, though, is to delay their first visit, thinking a young child won't recognize many of the objects displayed. But that is the most important reason for taking her: so she will encounter objects she doesn't know and hasn't seen before. Age two is not too early.

A second common error lies in not visiting the museum often enough. Two and three times a year isn't too often. Felicity will soon be racing excitedly from each familiar display or apparatus to the next one as if greeting old friends.

Even a war museum has a role to fill in her education when she is a little older. Here she will see a flintlock musket, a helmet, a shield, a sword, a scabbard, a spear and other items she may already have read about. Equip her with a pad and pencil so she can jot down the names of previously unknown items.

Museums, art galleries, conservatories, aquariums, exhibitions and fairs each provide their own fascinations. Look in the yellow pages of the telephone book. You may be surprised at the number of museums listed.

Some who live in cities never trouble to visit the attractions that are a visitor's first destination. Pick up a tourist guide to your city and take Felicity to see its attractions. .

Though television viewing takes youngsters into many buildings and settings, a TV picture isn't as interesting as a visit. The local fire station provides a captivating start for your program. Step in for a minute and let Felicity shake the hand of a real firefighter. If she mentions she doesn't play with matches the firefighter might take over and let her stand on the running board of the fire engine.

Step into the local police station and introduce Felicity to the officer on duty at the desk. Depending on how busy he is, the officer might chat about safety rules. He probably has children too and will be pleased to extend some fatherly advice.

Have you visited the public library with Felicity? If not, drop in occasionally so she will become accustomed to, and feel comfortable among, walls of books. And if she is now reading, stock up on reading material while you're there.

Visit the main train depot. The hustle and bustle will fascinate a child. Depending on the procedures observed, you might be able to take her onto the platform to inspect a train up close. A large bus depot provides its own interest. And perhaps the most riveting visit of all would be the airport. Explain the purpose of the control tower. Perhaps there is a windsock to guide pilots of smaller aircraft.

You may not be able to gain entry to the control tower, but if the meteorological office is situated in the airport complex, you might find a ready welcome there. If, after your visit to the airport, you can park on a road over which ascending or descending aircraft pass, Felicity will thrill to the noise and immensity of the planes.

If you live near a port, there will be a dock area to visit. The large ships, long wharves, their machinery and fittings will fill her with wonder.

A large farmer's market with its rich variety of produce, live rabbits and chickens, will captivate a youngster. And another kind of market, a flea market, will let Felicity see items not common in homes today: kerosene lamps, classical statues, and other antiquities.

Though you may have visited the supermarket several times with Felicity, have you ever visited its back door? Not only will she see the large trucks in the loading bays, she might have a peek at the ceiling-high stacks of food containers in the seldom seen warehouse area.

Let Felicity experience the unique sounds and smell of a lumberyard. Perhaps she will see a circular saw in operation.

A construction site – fascinating enough for adults – is awesome for a child. Visit a new building site where the bulldozers are working far below street level to clear out the subterranean floors. Then visit the site again periodically to let Felicity see each step as the structure gradually grows.

Visit the tallest building in your area and take the elevator to the top floor. The receptionist at some business there won't mind letting Felicity look out a window for a spectacular view.

Computers

The pioneer of motivation and learning, B.F. Skinner (who could train a pigeon to walk a figure eight in five minutes) perfected the teaching machine back in the late 1950s. Those are the humble roots from which today's high-tech computer programs have sprung. Not too relevant perhaps, but I thought I'd toss it in as a tribute to a rare educator.

The notion that learning is somehow stunted unless children have access to, and can operate, a computer is a fallacy schools have seized upon to convince disillusioned parents that education has now been rejuvenated by the advent of dazzling electronic software. Of course, this is not true. Education has steadily declined during the past seventy-five years.

Computers see little use at the Institute. A few computer programs have proven effective. When children are ready to begin typing, they should learn the 'touch' method. **Kid's Typing** by Sierra at **www.allstarreview.com** proved to be both efficient and highly entertaining. Children line up to use it. Several typing programs can be found simply by typing **Kid's Typing** into your search engine; a free typing program can be downloaded at **www.kidwaresoftware.com**

Math Blaster, by Davidson, holds pupils' attention and advances their computing skill. The producer, Davidson, along with forty other producers of children's educational programs can be accessed at the bottom of **www.smartkidssoftware.com**. From this same spot you can access Sunburst Communications whose *Hot Dog Stand: The Works* ingeniously sets a child up as proprietor of a hot dog stand and presents the various problems that must be dealt with to succeed in business. A free program dealing with the production and delivery of pizzas is available from **www.kidwaresoftware.com**. This site provides a number of free programs as well as many low cost programs.

An entire book could be written about the numerous educational programs now available for children. Fortunately, a book isn't needed. All the information can be readily found on the Internet. At **www.reviewcorner.com** more than 300 programs are described in detail. Ratings are given for their performance, the age for which each is suitable, the skills covered, their entertainment value, and cost.

Bear in mind, though, ages given are for children who haven't been advanced by parental effort and the program in this book.

Piano Lessons

Our interest in piano lessons is more than esthetic. A nine-month study conducted at the Royal Conservatory of Music by Dr. Glenn E. Schellenberg, University of Toronto at Mississauga, has shown that children advanced almost three IQ points more than non-participants. The activity is believed to strengthen parts of the brain employed in mathematics, spatial intelligence and general intellectual pursuits.

The children in the test were learning to play the piano by reading music. It seems, however, that even if children were not reading music, but merely plunking away in an attempt to create a melody, they would be similarly advancing their intelligence by exercising their problem-solving capability. A small child-size keyboard can be purchased for less than a couple of movie tickets (and provide longer, if less professional, entertainment).

17

Saving Your Schoolchild

What now of a child who received no special attention while in the womb, who was taught no academic subjects during the preschool years and who now, having entered public school, is performing below expectations? Is there any hope for this child?

Yes, indeed: but more than hope. Studies reveal a regenerative force in the brain that can effect both academic and intellectual advancement. Researchers at the University of California, Berkeley, have found changes take place in the brain when it is challenged. They found increases in the thickness and weight of the cerebral cortex or 'gray matter', and an increased size of neurons in the cortex, increased dendritic branching, increased number of dendritic spines per unit length of dendrite, increases in ... *but enough!* You get the picture. They found plasticity: a disposition on the part of the brain to change and grow if challenged.

Though the experiments were conducted with rats, gerbils, squirrels and monkeys, bogus thinking alone would lead us to believe the results would be different for humans. The message is clear – for four-legged animals and the two–legged type – the brain responds to work as if it were a muscle. By pumping iron – intellectually speaking – we generate brain growth.

But the best news is that intellectual advancement can begin at almost any age. Experiments confirm that when animals are introduced to a stimulating environment at an age equivalent to that of a seventy-five-year-old human, the same physical and chemical changes occur as are seen in younger animals. In the words of senior researcher Mark Rosenzweig, "The capacity for plastic neural changes was found to be present not only early in life but throughout most, if not all, of the life span."

If your child is younger than seventy-five, it seems your chances of rejuvenating his intellectual growth are high.

But will it take long? No. Astonishingly enough, it's fast. Neuroanatomist Marian Diamond found that intellectual enrichment produced chemical and structural changes in the brain in just four days. Later studies lowered the time to forty-five minutes. But lo! – even later studies proved that significant physiological changes take place almost instantly.

So, by getting your child – let's call him Boris – back on the rails academically and challenging his thinking, you will give him the equivalent of a brain massage.

How do you start?

That depends. First, why isn't he doing well in school?

One powerful force that contributes to academic failure is a child's opinion that he is "no good at" a subject, be it reading, mathematics, or perhaps anything associated with school work. Once such an idea has taken root in the child's mind it assumes the power of a hypnotically induced suggestion, and any improvement is unlikely until the child is led to see his conception of self is false.

Prescott Lecky's studies of self-induced academic failure, reported in the book *Self Consistency* (Shoe String Press), showed that improvement could be realized only by altering the pupil's state of mind, not by any promise of brighter business success.

Pupils failed in those subjects, Lecky found, in which they thought success was inconsistent with the image they held of themselves. (Perhaps why boys often fail at tasks they regard as feminine and girls fail at tasks they regard as masculine.) Lecky achieved success by convincing pupils there was no rational reason for continuing their self-deception and that success in a subject could be comfortably consistent with the image they held of themselves.

> *...we first explain to the pupil that his deficiency is not due to lack of ability, but to a standard which he created himself. We must make it clear that the standard is unconscious, since this explains why he has continued to maintain it. It is most important that the interpretation of his difficulty be offered in a friendly and uncritical manner. The attitude should be that this is not our problem, but his.*

Next, Lecky strengthened the student's concept of self-reliance, independence, and the ability to solve his problem by his own effort.

Finally, the student was led to see – without criticism – the inconsistency of his thinking between mature and immature standards.

How effective was this treatment?

> *A high school student who misspelled 55 words out of a hundred, and who failed so many subjects that he lost credit for a full year, became one of the best spellers in the school during the next year, and made a general average of 91. A student who was dropped from another college and was later admitted to Columbia was graduated with more than 70 points of "A" credits. A boy failing in English, who had been diagnosed by a testing bureau as lacking aptitude for this subject, won honorable mention a year later for the literary prize at a large preparatory school. A girl who had failed four times in Latin, with marks between 20 and 50, after three talks with the school counselor made a mark of 92 on the next test and finished with a grade of 84. She is now taking advanced Latin with grades above 80.*

Such is the magic of correcting a flawed inner vision. Such is the wonder of awaking a student from his comfortable cocoon of failure.

But now, back to Boris. Let's suppose the youngster is having trouble reading – a fairly common complaint. His problem may be more than a faulty self-image. The ability to read depends on knowing important mechanical details; for example, the letter code.

To find out how well Boris knows the code have him read the test material on page 86. If he can't read these words easily, then all the self-confidence in the world isn't going to make him read skillfully. He will have to go through the reading program presented in Chapter 7 and learn what he hasn't been taught. That could be quite a trial – right?

Fortunately, we can sweeten this procedure in a way that will not only build his self-confidence and self-esteem, but will reward him with extra pocket money. How?

Have Boris teach another child to read!

It works this way. Find someone – a neighbor or a friend – with a preschooler Boris can teach to read. Explain to Boris that Mrs. So-and-so wants her preschooler to begin reading and she will pay Boris X cents/dollars for each lesson he gives. (You would reimburse your neighbor for the amount she appears to pay him.)

Next, convince Boris that he can handle the job with your help. This means you would teach Boris in simple steps – steps he would immediately teach his pupil – the program presented in Chapter 7. This procedure will oblige Boris to repeat the letter sounds with you, and then with his pupil. He will get an earful of letter-sounds and will become skillful in using them. And, of course, when the preschooler is able to read, Boris will be reading too.

You may have to pay out a sizeable amount of money, but think, this is cheaper than paying for professional tutoring. And it will be far more interesting and effective. I'll bet there is some (relatively) expensive item Boris would be eager to buy. Suddenly, he will be highly motivated to earn its purchase price.

By this same method, called *Each One Teach One,* Frank Laubach, an evangelical missionary working in the Phillipines, taught an estimated sixty million people to read (which makes the rest of us look like dabblers).

There is still one problem to address. What if Boris is dyslexic?

I weep to think of the many children who have been cheated out of the wonders of reading by affixing this label to them. When the experts – usually educational psychologists – attribute a reading difficulty to dyslexia everyone escapes blame. Teachers are let off the hook. School administrators raise their hands futilely and extend condolences to distraught parents. And the child, unfortunately, is sentenced to a life devoid of printed enjoyment. I expand upon this dishonest practice in my book *Teach Your Child to Read in Just Ten Minutes a Day* in an appendix entitled *The Myth of Dyslexia.* I will mention it briefly here.

Thousands of children have passed through the Ledson Institute. Every one has learned to read. If there are dyslexics, how can it be that we have never seen one? Top-notch public school teachers report the same surprising absence of dyslexic children. Ask around in your city or town. You are bound to find one or two teachers who have never encountered a child who couldn't learn to read. You will also find that all of these 'lucky' teachers used a reading program that stressed learning the letter sounds.

All manner of reasons are given for children supposedly being afflicted with dyslexia: their diet, their genes, their heaven-knows-what, and researchers stubbornly refuse – with a persistence that makes granite look flexible – to address the fact that when children are correctly taught, dyslexia vanishes.

Schoolchildren who attend the remedial reading clinic at the Institute report all manner of deficiencies they supposedly suffer from that prevent their learning to read well. Our teachers introduce them to the letter code, show them how to use it, practice them in using it, and their mysterious ailments vanish as if by magic. I have watched this happen for twenty-five years now.

> Further instructions for helping school-age children who are reading poorly (or seldom) are presented in my book *Teach Your Child to Read in Just Ten Minutes a Day*. Other sections show kindergarten and elementary grade teachers, nursery school teachers and daycare attendants how to achieve the same 100% reading success teachers achieve at the Institute. Babysitters, too, learn how to provide an unrivalled service in their neighborhood by teaching their young charges to read.

Enticing Reading

Television viewers are occasionally required to read. But Boris, probably an ardent TV viewer, must read more often than occasionally if he is to become a skillful, adventurous reader. Plenty of fascinating reading material should be available in the home to lure him away from the TV set. In fact, TV viewing might be made conditional upon his reading for a stated length of time. (One minute of television viewing for each minute of reading?) In one home where this program was introduced, the child became so interested in the reading he forgot to turn on the television set. For more ways to promote reading, see Chapter 8.

Other Problems

But what if Boris has a problem with mathematics? Assuredly, the laws of mathematics provide ample opportunity for confusion in a child's mind, especially if the teacher has moved ahead too quickly or explained the rules ineptly. Once confusion has taken hold, uncertainty and loss of confidence take over, and the child approaches the same mental swamp that captured the poor reader.

The solution lies in giving a child plenty of practice at each early level of math; and because mathematics doesn't provide the built-in rewards that can be found in reading (by the entertainment inherent in text) you may have to provide some extrinsic reward, as described in Chapter 7.

Whatever subject Boris is failing in, or the reason for his failing, complaint to the school will usually achieve little. Parents forget that schools are not obliged to teach children anything. They are obliged to *try*. And if they fail, excuses can always be found to transfer blame to the child or to the home. Be warned.

If you suspect poor reading ability is contributing to Boris' aversion to learning, have him take the literacy test on page 86.

The Vitamin C Boost

In a study reported by Kubala and Katz, blood samples of students ranging from kindergarten to college were used to distinguish those students having high ascorbic acid (vitamin C) in their blood, and those having low ascorbic acid levels. Seventy-two pairs of high and low vitamin students were then formed – each member of the pair coming from homes with similar family income and parent education. The group having the higher ascorbic acid level tested 4.51 IQ points higher than the lower ascorbic acid group. Both groups then received supplementary orange juice during a six-month period. Though the IQ of the high achievers rose little, the lower group experienced an increase of 3.54 IQ units. A second study the following year produced similar results.

The Question of Happiness

Happiness consists more in small conveniences or pleasures that occur every day, than in great pieces of good fortune that happen but seldom to a man in the course of his life.

Benjamin Franklin

Imagine the worry that must burden a wealthy person when he finds teredos boring through the hull of his luxury yacht. Wouldn't we all like to have that sort of worry? Putting aside the supposed delights of wealth for the moment, the rich man's worry is no less than yours or mine when we discover someone has dinged a fender of our car. Worry comes in all shapes and sizes suited to the highest and the lowest. Anyone who thinks the occupants of Buckingham Palace and the White House revel in never-ending happiness is a prospect for swamp property ownership in Florida.

Why all this concern with happiness?

Because critics are quick to claim that high intelligence doesn't guarantee happiness. And they're right, it doesn't. As a rule, brilliant people are no happier than anyone else. Yet happiness is more important than intellectual brilliance or professional success, so it behooves you to give young Mario some additional guidance to prevent his brilliance becoming his millstone.

High intelligence, like wealth and physical strength, is a power. And power, ineptly used, is abusive. The characteristics that allow children to make friends easily are learned largely by the example their parents set. Children will have more or less respect for others, for their rights and property, and they will be more or less prone to gentleness, kindness and generosity to whatever extent they see these traits valued

and exemplified by their parents. Even a child's concept of honesty –
interpreted differently from home to home – will be established mainly
by parental example.

This is not the place for a sermon. Every thinking adult knows that if
one is to attract affection, admiration, respect, and loyalty – the
requisites for a happy life – one must be affectionate, admirable,
respectful, loyal, *and humble*. No one likes a braggart. A brilliant child
too easily becomes a conceited child, and a child with an inflated
opinion of his own worth will be burdened with a social disadvantage
that far outweighs any intellectual advantage he has gained.

Patience

Those with quick minds have trouble understanding why others have
difficulty dealing with problems. While the average person gropes his
way slowly through a problem, the active mind has raced ahead, defined
and resolved the issue, and waits, perhaps restlessly, for the slower
person to catch up. Unless the bright child learns to demonstrate
tolerance and patience, his life, both as a youngster and as an adult can
be frustrating.

Compliment

If we draw children's attention to examples of desirable conduct, we
prompt them to emulate that conduct. "Look, Mario, that man with all
the parcels couldn't open the door, so the lady came back and opened it
for him. Isn't that nice? She's kind and thoughtful. There are some nice
people around, aren't there?"

Even better, if we teach children to voice their approval when they
see a personal trait or action they like, we equip them with a universally
valued gift: the art of compliment. How often have you or I seen
something praiseworthy when, because of an inbred or conditioned
restraint, we have failed to mention our approval? When a child is
awakened to the fact that other people appreciate compliments just as
much as he does, he becomes eligible for an important lesson in making
friends. Practice might start at home: "Mommy cooked a delicious
supper, right, Mario?" Let's hear it for the cook. Hip-hip ..."

When children see the pleasure their words of appreciation arouse,
they will warm to the procedure. In fact, encouraging children to
express their appreciation may help parents overcome their own
inhibition about giving compliment: an inhibition possibly based on a
fear of rebuff or a fear their compliment may be misinterpreted.

If Mario is now able to print, engage him in an exercise that employs
compliment. Pick someone you both know or have observed – a friend,

a relative, a neighbor, or perhaps even a salesclerk – and help him compose a list of that person's likable traits or characteristics.

PARENT: What do you think of the lady at the information booth at the shopping mall, Mario?
CHILD: She looks nice.
PARENT: Yes, well that's because she's *neat*. And that means everything about her is tidy. Put down *neat*. [Spell it.] Anything else?
CHILD: She smiles a lot.
PARENT : Right. She's *pleasant*. Print it. Anything else?
CHILD: She asked me why my hand was bandaged.
PARENT: Yes. She's *concerned* about others. And that's because she is *kind* and *considerate*.

With a little help, Mario will be able to list several pleasing features seen in the person you are describing. What if, on your next visit to the shopping center, he were to hand his list to the lady? The list might top her day, if not her entire year, and would probably be displayed on her refrigerator at home for a long time.

By engaging Mario a few times – why not once a week? – in a game of "Let's Say Something Nice about ….," or whatever you wish to call it, he will not only brighten people's lives, he will become sensitized to other people's commendable features. Most important, of course, he will become practiced in the art of dispensing appreciation.

Absence of Fears

Children are more likely to be happy and adventurous if their lives are free of fears. Parental fears are too easily passed to youngsters: fear of snakes, insects, and bats. If you live in an area where dangerous creatures roam, Mario must be warned; but the common house spider or moth is harmless, so why instill an abhorrence of the creatures? If you can't bring yourself to pick up a caterpillar or snail with your bare fingers, be sure not to show revulsion when Mario picks one up. Someday you may be thankful to have some fearless person handy to pick up and remove such creatures from the house for you.

A particularly thoughtless fear, induced as a joke, is to frighten a child by the supposed presence of a monster in the closet or under the bed: a fear that, once induced, is difficult to erase because having taught a child to fear something that doesn't exist, the parent has little means, later, of proving the creature is nonexistent.

These, then, are a few ways to help ensure Mario's life will be a little happier; though never neglecting the all important fact that – and here we should sound the trumpets – happiness is mainly an attitude or state of mind. Abe Lincoln hit it right when he said people are just about as happy as they make up their mind to be. We can all drum up good reasons for being gloomy and list the various ways fate has short-changed us. Possibly some folks have valid reason to complain about their lot. If you are sleeping at night on a warm-air street grating then, it's true, you have a reasonable argument for feeling and looking glum.

An old song, *Painting the Clouds with Sunshine*, suggested a remedy for making the best of a sad situation: wear a smile. A vivid picture of brightness in the wake of adversity was described in Dale Carnegie's book *How to Win Friends and Influence People*. Here is the way he described it.

> *I was walking up the stairs of the Long Island station in New York. Directly in front of me thirty or forty crippled boys on canes and crutches were struggling up the stairs. One boy had to be carried up. I was astonished at their laughter and gaiety. I spoke about it to one of the men in charge of the boys. "Oh, yes," he said, "when a boy realizes that he is going to be a cripple for life, he is shocked at first; but, after he gets over the shock, he usually resigns himself to his fate and then becomes happier than normal boys."*

Everyone is crippled in some way. We may have full use of our legs yet some other adversity – seemingly large to us but perhaps not to others – catches the tail of one or two other grievances and creates a composite disability that seems as punishing as the loss of a limb. Would you banish all your worries for the loss of a leg? Everyone can make a conscious choice to be glum, or to be happy, or to be something in between.

Now, if you want to give your child a rare gift – almost like icing on the cake of intellectual brilliance that you've already equipped him with – give him a sense of humor. It's worth a million dollars. No, make that two million.

Sense of Humor

The term 'sense of humor' is frequently misunderstood. The ability to laugh at a joke or comic situation doesn't mean someone has a sense of humor. Anyone can laugh when presented with comic material. Having a sense of humor lies in the ability to discern droll possibilities in everyday situations: seeing humor where it isn't obvious or intended.

Fortunately, a sense of humor can be developed. Not overnight, of course, but with practice. Not only would you be assuring young Mario a happier life, you would be assuring him a *healthier* life.

Getting technical for a moment, our health is seen to be largely controlled by our emotions. Humor increases both the activity and number of natural killer cells and helper T-cells; and at the same time, humor reduces stress hormones and boosts other complex substances that influence the likelihood of our staying well. In short, humor creates a circulatory healing soup. Muscles relax when humor abounds. Studies show that those individuals with a better sense of humor have stronger immune systems: a matter tested and proved by Norman Cousins who, by employing humor, boosted his body's defense system sufficiently to save his life: recorded in his book, *Anatomy of an Illness*.

You can give Mario this special gift by sensitizing him to comedy. When he possesses a sense of humor, he won't be dependent upon chance encounters for his yuks. He will carry comedy with him and be able to create hilarity whenever he wishes.

How do you get him started? Simple. Teach him a few jokes. This will lead him to see matters with a comic view that spells fun. Depending on Mario's age, the following jokes may be suitable for springing on Daddy, Grandma, or anyone else he meets. Of course, he himself will double up with laughter while telling the joke but his delicious giggle will add to the fun. Start him with a few elephant jokes.

What time is it when an elephant sits on a fence?
Time to fix the fence!

Policeman: "One of your elephants has been seen
chasing a man on a bicycle."
Zoo Keeper: "Nonsense, none of my elephants
know how to ride a bicycle!"

Teacher: "Name six wild animals."
Pupil: "Four elephants and two lions."

How do you know when there's an elephant under
your bed?
When your nose touches the ceiling.

You will find hundreds of jokes at *www.jokesnjokes.net*. Check the **kids jokes** subsection.

And because you've been patient and haven't fidgeted, here's one for you.

What's big and gray and lives in a lake in Scotland?

The Loch Ness Elephant

Appendix 1

Here are some of the children who have secured early intellectual superiority by participation in the program on which this book is based. Reading levels were determined in one of two ways depending on the child's age. One method employed an early version of the Gray Oral Reading Test in use at a time when reading skills were more severely judged. A second assessment was obtained by reference to the public school grade-level ratings assigned to books the children were then able to read (admittedly a less accurate reference because of the wide variation that exists in reading ability between schools).

> *Primer* – Grade 1
> *First Reader* (96 sentences) – Grade 1-2
> *Second Reader* – Grade 2-3

After three years at the Institute, **Laurence Batmazian**, age 6, could read 100-page books without stopping. In an endorsement of the Institute memory-training program, his parents reported, "He always impresses people with his ability to discuss subjects in a very mature manner, remembers conversations and discussions with an enviable recollection of what was said and done by who and where."

Mitchell Au, age 2, couldn't speak English when he entered the Institute. After seven months of half-day attendance, he was reading the *First Reader*.

After attending three half-days a week for four months, followed by five half-days a week, **Stephen Zhao**, age 2, was reading the *First Reader*. By age 6, his reading had advanced to a Grade 6 level: equivalent to a child age 11.

Vivian Podorojansky, age 4, spoke only Russian when she began the Institute program. Eight months later, Vivian was reading the *Second Reader*.

Jeremy Wong, age 3, couldn't speak English on enrolment. Four months later, he completed the *First Reader*.

In four months, **Jalia Kanji**, age 3, read the *First Reader* and demonstrated a new and surprising ability to converse with adults.

After attending the Institute for four years, seven-year-old **Nelson Zhang** was reading and functioning at a Grade 11 level – at the level of a child age 16.

Neena Allidina, age 4, read 13 books during our Readathon. At that time, Neena was reading the science text *Gorillas*, rated Grade 3.

In five months, **Daniel Tao**, age 3, was reading the *First Reader*. He could also add and subtract (both of which he loved). By age 7, Daniel was reading at a Grade 11 level.

A month after enrolling, **Eric Furtado**, age 2, had progressed to the *Second Reader*. Three months later, his reading had advanced to the level of a seven-year-old. Mr. and Mrs. Furtado reported, "He surprises not only us but others around him, not just with his extensive vocabulary, but also when he starts to read complicated words and books that his much older peers are unable to."

After two years, **Tamara Zimmerman**, then age 4, was reading Grade 4 material. Two years later, Tamara was reading books of 40,000-word length.

Jessica Li spoke no English on enrolment. She completed the *Primer* and was reading the *First Reader* while still age 2.

By the time **Mark Lazarte** reached age 4, he was able to read the newspaper, add two-digit numbers, and solve difficult mazes.

In twelve months, **Rabya Gillani**, age 3, was reading at a Grade 3 level.

Shamit Bhagani, age 3, was reading the *Second Reader* in five months.

When **Sarah Weiss** had been in the program for thirteen months, her mother reported that Sarah, then five, read A.A.Milne's *The World of Pooh*, not missing even the introduction, and she read almost anything around the house, including the TV Guide. Sarah's math skills had progressed to fractions and she was becoming highly competent in using the dictionary – an activity she loved.

186

Shun Yao advanced to a Grade 2 text while still in our kindergarten. A year later, then age six, he was reading at almost a Grade 5 level.

In just two months, **Andrew Campion**, age 4, was halfway through the *First Reader*.

Alyssa Pandolfo read the *Primer* and moved on to the *First Reader* while still age 2.

Though attending only two half days a week, **Aliya Ismail**, age 3, was reading Grade 2 material three months later.

Appendix 2

How will you be able to tell if your child achieves an IQ of 140?

The inclusion of an IQ test here is not possible; therefore, we must find other ways to assess your child's advancing intelligence. Of first importance is your child's demonstrated maturity of manner and abilities when compared with other children the same age: observations that, surprisingly, can sometimes provide a more convincing assessment of intelligence than those derived by paper tests because IQ tests differ in their results. To illustrate, a score of 131 on the Ravens Standard Matrices is equivalent to 148 on the Wechsler Scale: an intriguing seventeen point variation that leads us to believe psychometrics (the measurement of intelligence) is more an art, than a science. The scores reached by such tests are therefore merely *estimates* of intelligence; estimates that are closer to reality depending on which test you happen to use.

Though IQ test results are speculative, observations of children's ability and manner is real, unswerving, and definable. A bright child is clearly distinguishable by his or her conduct. How much brighter that child is than an average child is estimable – and likely to afford less than a seventeen-point error.

The chart on the next page shows how a child would function in demonstrating an IQ of 140. Ages shown across the bottom are the child's actual age. Those shown up the left side indicate the child's intellectual age. The diagonal line indicates the functional performance of a child with an IQ of 140.

Determined mathematically, a child age two – indicated at the lower left corner – would have to function as a child age two years, nine-and-a-half-months. A child age three would have to perform in the manner of a child age four years, two-and-a-half-months. A child age four would have to perform in the manner of a child five years, seven months. At age five, the child's performance would equal that of a child seven years, one-half month. At age six, achievement would equal that of a child eight years, four months. Ages lying between these points can be assessed by running a line up to the diagonal.

The level at which children are reading contributes fairly to an assessment of the child's intellectual ability. If a three-year-old is able to read and understand material written for Grade 2 public school children (age seven), this would confirm an uncommonly high level of intellectual achievement.

Lest educators not agree with these postulations, an elaboration might be appropriate. The usual methods of measuring intelligence are, as we have seen, but loosely scientific. Individuals with measurable high intelligence sometimes act in less than brilliant ways. Conversely, those with proven high intelligence sometimes score low on IQ tests: a memorable instance is seen in the case of Henri Poincaré, the French mathematical genius.

Poincaré, leading man in science during the 20th century, possessed a photographic memory – an astonishing ability to recall the page and line of any information he had read. When he submitted to an IQ test, he scored so low that if a child had achieved the same score, the child would have been classified as an imbecile.

Genius intelligence does not rest wholly with the possession of a high IQ score. Genius intelligence is an observed intellectual ability – of the sort amply demonstrated by the children described in Appendix 1: a cerebrally elevated group of youngsters we hope your child will soon join.

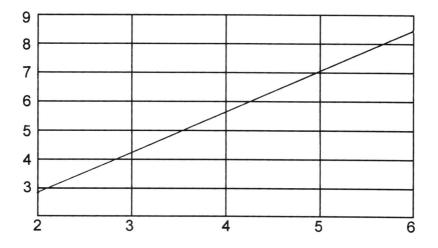

Figure 28: Chart showing relationship of age and performance.

Index

Able Misfits, 51
Academy of Medical Sciences
    (USSR), 31
adjectives, 97
alcohol, dangers of, 20, 21
Alger, Ferris, 13
American Way of Birth, The, 22
Anatomy of an Illness, The, 183
Astaire, Fred, 158
Azrin, Nathan H., 34

babysitters as tutors, 47
Beethoven, 18
Bell, Alexander Graham, 164
Bennett, William J., 40
Bentham, Jeremy, 4, 5, 8
Berle, Adolf, 7, 8
Berle, Adolf Jr., 8
bilingualism, 44
Boyer, Ernest, 156
Brahms, 18

Caesarian section, 21
caffeine, dangers of, 21
Carnegie, Dale, 182
Casparov, Gary, 2
catecholamines, 20
Children Who Read Early, 39
Churchill, Winston, 40
Churchill Heights Public
School,   161
Columbia Law School, 8
comic books, 88
computers, 171
convenience education, 45-49
Cousins, Norman, 183
Cox, Catherine M., 11
Cradles of Eminence, 51

Curie, Maria, 9
cybernetics, 8

Devaluing of America, The, 40
Diamond, Marion, 175
Dick and Jane reading program,
    87
Diligent Spotter, 143
Durkin, Dolores, 39, 51, 161
dyslexia, 176

Edison, Thomas, 128
education – while eating, 45, 46
            – while traveling, 46
            – while shopping, 46
Education of Karl Witte, The, 7
Einstein, Albert, 2, 9, 13, 43,
44
encyclopedias, 88, 89
Escondido, California, 16

Fisher, Bobby, 2
Franklin, Benjamin, 179
Foxx, Richard M., 34

Gates, Bill, 2,
*Genetic Studies of Genius,
    Volume   II*, 11
Gesellschaft für Rationelle
    Psychologie, 30
Goertzel & Goertzel, 51
Graham, Robert, 16
grammar, 148-151
Greek prose authors, 6
Green, family, 3, 4, 8, 9
Grog, Stanislav, 19
Grosvenor, Gilbert, 164
Growing Without Schooling,
164

Printed in the United States
By Bookmasters